REPRODUCIBLE

D1430366

FAITH BUILDERS

BIBLE CRAFTS FOR CHILDREN
AGES 7-10

NADIA HERBERT

Abingdon Press

FAITH BUILDERS

Written by Nadia Herbert

Designed and Illustrated by Paige Easter

ISBN 978-0-687-64361-5

08 09 10 11 12 13 14 15 16 17—10 9 8 7 6 5 4 3 2 1

Manufactured in the United States of America.

TABLE OF CONTENTS
CRAFT AND THEME

3

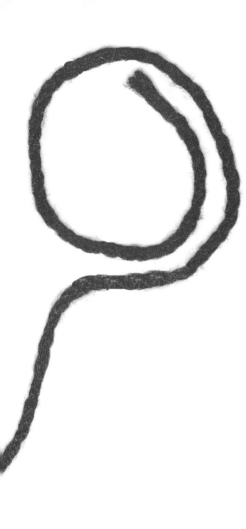

INTRODUCTION

FAITH BUILDERS is a children's ministry resource, containing a whole year of Sunday school teaching in one book. It features fifty exciting craft projects that children will enjoy making while learning about the Bible and building their faith. Each craft has a theme that is linked to a related Bible verse and combined with a complete lesson.

For the teacher, there are clear, step-by-step instructions to follow, along with a materials list and an indication of the time needed to complete the project. Crafts include a bird feeder, seashell wind chimes, and even a marshmallow caterpillar!

FAITH BUILDERS utilizes many wonderful media through which children can express their creativity and explore their faith in a group setting. This ready-to-use book provides a hands-on, fun way of bringing God's Word to children that will maintain their enthusiasm for Sunday school.

CRAFT NOTES

All the crafts in this book are made from materials that are easy to obtain and inexpensive. They have been designed with the limitations of a church budget in mind. Most of the materials are available from large discount warehouses or chain stores.

- Air-drying clay is available in packs of different sizes. It takes twenty-four hours to dry at room temperature. Leftover clay can be stored indefinitely in cling wrap in a cool place.

- Play dough can be made at home from a recipe (see pages 57 and 97). All dough crafts must be varnished to repel moisture.

- Felt can be purchased on a roll from large craft and fabric stores.

A list of requirements is given for each individual craft, but other useful items are

- clean jars or ice cream containers for washing brushes during painting activities;

- a good supply of old newspapers and paper towels;

- rags for clean up and spills;

- plastic sheeting (available from hardware stores) to protect desks/tables;

- aprons/art shirts or other protective clothing;

- a pair of left-handed scissors.

SAFETY PRECAUTIONS

Insure the children are supervised at all times. Wipe up spills immediately, particularly on the floor. Use non-toxic glues, paints, and markers. Insure adequate ventilation when using varnish or strong-smelling glue. Always supervise the use of spray cans and hot glue guns. Make sure to keep any potentially dangerous equipment, such as craft knives, out of sight and out of reach. Have a first aid kit available. Demonstrate to older children how to use a glue gun safely, and warn them to be careful of the liquid glue as it is very hot. Do not allow younger children to use a glue gun.

1. PHOTO TREE
OUR CHURCH FAMILY

Children can discuss the importance of belonging to the church community while making this "family" tree.

PREPARATION

You will need to have photos of your Sunday school class, congregation, worship leaders, church building, and so forth ready for this craft. (Every child will need to have one of each photo.)

1. Choose a volunteer to read the Bible verse to the class. Explain that it refers to the church congregation. The Bible tells us about the first Christians and how they were like an ever-growing family. They often met together to pray, share food, worship, give money to the poor, and to help and guide each other. Tell the children that attending church pleases God. Church is a special place where we worship and praise God. We have many reasons for attending church, such as to feel close to God, pray with other Christians, learn about God and Jesus, make friends, and be with people who care about us.

2. Explain that Christians are all part of God's family. The rest of our "family" are all other believers. By being members of the church congregation, we know we are important and secure in this special family. We are also showing our commitment to serving God, and regular attendance helps make our commitment stronger.

3. Explain that the church community is like a flourishing tree, blossoming and growing all the time. Distribute the craft materials for making a photo tree. Encourage the children to think about the value of their church family as they make their photo trees. Show them how to draw a tree shape similar to the one pictured here on a piece of brown felt. Have them cut it out and glue it onto construction paper. Have them cut carefully

BIBLE READING
Hebrews 10:24-25
(CEV)

TIME REQUIRED
40 minutes

MATERIALS
construction paper
(one large sheet per child)

brown felt

scraps of green felt

craft glue

scissors

pencils

photos
(see preparation)

around the edges of each photo to remove the corners and any unnecessary background. Then they can glue the photos onto the tree branches and trunk. Next, show them how to cut out small leaves from green felt and glue these around the photos and on the branches. As the children work on their craft, discuss how church is a place where we are always welcome. It gives us a feeling of belonging, and the church is somewhere we can focus on God in the company of Christian friends.

4. When the children have completed their photo trees, talk with them about ways they can be more involved with the church. Suggest helping younger children, joining the choir, being a greeter, helping serve the refreshments, handing out hymn books, joining a Bible study group, or helping the elderly to their seats. Conclude the lesson by reading the prayer.

PRAYER

Dear God, please be with our church family and keep us all strong in our commitment to you. Amen.

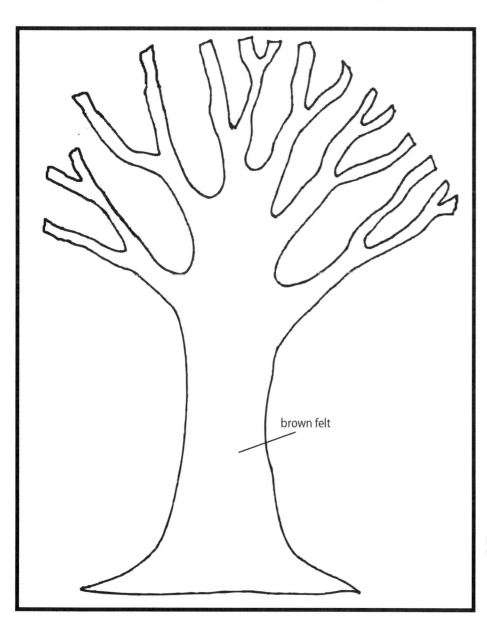

brown felt

2. MOSAIC PICTURE
OUR VIEW OF GOD

Creating this mosaic picture will encourage children to think about who God is.

1. Read the Bible passage to the children. Ask the children if they have a picture in their minds of what God is like. How does God appear to them? Explain that some people think of God with a human body, while others think of God as a presence around them. The Bible tells us that God is a spirit, which means that God is invisible but that God is close to each one of us.

2. Tell the children that the Bible describes God's personality and qualities, and the more they study it, the more they will understand who God is. Ask them to read carefully through Psalm 103:1-10 (CEV). Write each of God's characteristics on a large piece of paper as expressed in the Bible passage: kind, forgiving, healing, loving, merciful, generous, fair, slow to anger, patient, and understanding.

3. Give out the craft materials and invite the children to make a mosaic picture of how they imagine God. Show the children how to draw their picture first on white construction paper. They can then fill in the drawing with small pieces of tissue paper rolled into balls and glued on. Any detail can be added afterwards with colored markers.

4. Encourage the children to think about God's personality as they create their mosaic picture. Remind them of the following points:

God wants to share love with everyone;

God is generous and fills our lives with good things;

God keeps promises and we can trust God;

BIBLE READING
Psalm 103:1-10 (CEV)

TIME REQUIRED
40 minutes

MATERIALS
large piece of paper

white construction paper
(one sheet per child)

scissors

colored markers

glue sticks

tissue paper
(assorted colors)

pencils

God is patient and forgiving when we make mistakes;
God is fair and dislikes injustice.

5. Talk with the children individually as they work on their pictures. Allow time at the end for those who want to share their work with the class. When everyone has finished, display the pictures. Ask for a volunteer to read the prayer.

PRAYER
Almighty Father, we know you are a wonderful God. We love and respect everything about you. Amen.

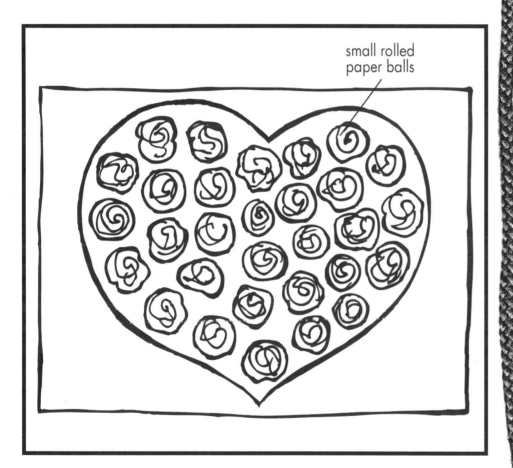

small rolled paper balls

3. SHEEP WALL DECORATION

KNOWING JESUS LEADS US TO GOD

This friendly sheep will help children understand that Jesus leads us to God.

BIBLE READING
John 10:1-11

TIME REQUIRED
40 minutes

MATERIALS

p. 108
large piece of paper
marker
cotton balls
glue sticks
tissue paper
(black and pink)

PREPARATION

Before class begins, photocopy the sheep face and ears (p. 108) for each child.

1. Copy the following references onto a large piece of paper and ask the children to look them up in their Bibles: Hebrews 13:20, Matthew 9:36, 1 Peter 2:25, Psalm 23:1, John 10:27-30. From these passages, they can see how Jesus is frequently referred to as a shepherd and that the "sheep" he lovingly cares for are God's people. Explain that a shepherd is someone who takes care of sheep. It is a shepherd's job to protect the sheep from harm, watch over them, and lead them to safety.

2. Read John 10:1-11 aloud to the children. Explain that it tells us we must follow Jesus because Jesus leads us to God.

3. Distribute the photocopies and craft materials. Invite the children to make a wall decoration of a sheep's face to display at home as a reminder that Jesus is "The Good Shepherd." Have the children cut out the face and ears. Show them how to stick the cotton balls onto the faces with the glue sticks. Have them glue on the ears. Have them make small balls of black tissue paper for the eyes and small balls of pink for the nose.

4. **A**s the children make their sheep, ask them to think about the many things Jesus taught us, such as:

to love and obey God

how to pray

how to treat other people

to be forgiving

to show love and kindness to everyone

how to please God

5. **W**hen the children have made their sheep, ask them to tell you the important things a shepherd did to care for his sheep. Then ask them to tell you the important things Jesus has done for us. Ask for a volunteer to read the prayer.

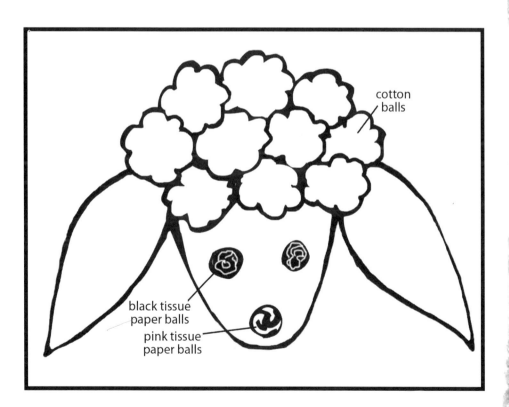

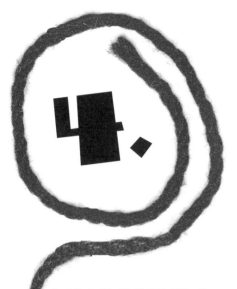
4.

BOARD GAME
USING THE BIBLE TO GUIDE US

Children will learn how the Bible can help them in life as they make this board game.

PREPARATION

Photocopy the page of Bible references (p. 108) and the checkerboard pattern (p. 109) for each child.

1. Ask a volunteer to read Psalm 32:8 to the class. Explain that one reason God gave us God's Word, the Bible, is so we can make wise choices in life. Emphasize how important it is to read our Bibles on a regular basis. Reading the Bible each day will help us to know God better and grow closer to God. Tell the children that they should pray before reading their Bibles and ask God to help them understand what they are reading.

2. Ask the children what we can learn from the Bible. Write their responses on a large piece of paper. Include that the Bible

    shows us right from wrong

    gives us good advice

    tells us what the future holds

    gives us knowledge about God and Jesus

    teaches us how to please God

    tells of God's love for us

3. Give each child a copy of the checkerboard. Have colored markers, paper, and pens for everyone to use. Explain that the game they are going to make represents their lives, with all the challenges they may encounter. It also represents the good things in life. Draw a diagram on a large piece of paper showing how they should make their games. Write a statement on each

BIBLE READING
Psalm 32:8

TIME REQUIRED
40 minutes

MATERIALS

pp. 108 and 109

two large pieces of paper

colored markers

counters and dice (sufficient quantity for everyone to play their games)

paper and pens

white square. For example, on the first white square, write "Did a good deed. Go forward three spaces." The player should then find a Bible verse for kindness before moving forward. Some squares should have negatives, such as "Told a lie. Go back to start." The player should then go back to the start and find a Bible verse for honesty.

4. **S**uggest the children work in pairs or small groups to brainstorm and write their ideas on paper first before writing on the board game. Give help with spelling and grammar. Allow fifteen minutes for planning, then a few minutes for transferring it to the game board. When the games are complete, divide the class into pairs and give each pair a die, two counters and a page of Bible references (p. 108). Explain that they can now play their games, looking up the relevant Bible verses as they go.

5. **T**his is a good way for children to become familiar with the Bible in a fun environment. Allow twenty minutes for the children to play their board games. Remind them that by following God's teaching in the Bible, they can have a good and happy life. Ask everyone to think of something new they have learned from the Bible today. Conclude the lesson with the prayer.

PRAYER
Dear God,
help us to
understand your
teaching as your
Word guides us
through life. Amen.

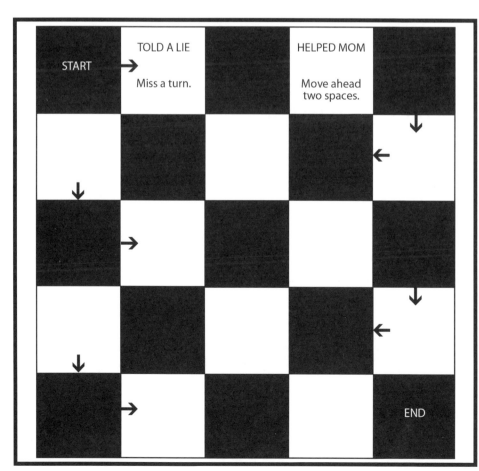

5. PRAYER BOOK
ENCOURAGING PERSONAL PRAYER

This personal prayer book will encourage children to keep in touch with God.

BIBLE READING
Matthew 6:9-13

TIME REQUIRED
40 minutes

MATERIALS

shiny gold cardstock
(8- by 6-inches)
one piece per child

colored cardstock
(8- by 6-inches)
six pieces per child

scissors

paper punch

ribbon or yarn
(one 8-inch piece per child)

pens

colored markers

craft scissors
(to cut decorative edges)

1. Display the words of the Lord's Prayer (p. 17) and show where it occurs in Matthew 6:9-13. Tell the children that they will be able to say it with you at the end of the lesson.

2. Start the lesson by explaining that Jesus used this prayer to teach his disciples what to say when they prayed. Explain that personal prayers are important for everyone who wants to know God.

3. Ask the children if they know what to say when they pray. Do they have difficulty finding the right words? Explain that it can help to write down the things we pray for. Having our own prayer book can help us pray more. It can be used as a prayer journal to note any special requests, such as a prayer for healing a sick relative.

4. Hand out the gold cardstock, colored cardstock, paper punch, scissors, and ribbon or yarn. Show the children how to use the colored cardstock as pages, and the gold cardstock as a cover for their prayer book. Have them carefully align the pages and cover, then use the paper punch on the left side to make two holes. Some children may need help with this. Show them how to thread the ribbon or yarn through the holes to secure the pages and cover together. Knot the ribbon or yarn firmly on the top of the cover to complete the prayer book. Decorate the cover. Trim the cover and pages with craft scissors to make decorative edges.

5. As the children make their prayer books, discuss some of the following aspects of prayer: God listens to our spoken prayers and hears our silent ones too. When we pray, we are talking directly to God. We can be totally honest when we pray. God will listen and answer wisely if we are being faithful. We must not be selfish or greedy when we pray.

6. When the children have finished decorating their books, suggest they copy the Lord's Prayer onto the first page. Explain that the Lord's Prayer is the model we can use when we pray. Remind them that prayer helps us grow closer to God. Invite the children to choose a special time to pray every day, such as bedtime, mealtime, or when they first get up each morning.

7. Allow the children time to write down any prayer requests they have. Explain that we can pray to praise God, to ask for forgiveness, to thank God, to ask for the things we need, and to pray for others. Conclude by saying the Lord's Prayer together.

PRAYER

Our Father, who art in heaven, hallowed be thy name. Thy kingdom come, thy will be done on earth as it is in heaven. Give us this day our daily bread. And forgive us our trespasses, as we forgive those who trespass against us. And lead us not into temptation, but deliver us from evil. For thine is the kingdom, and the power, and the glory, forever. Amen.

Our Father, who art in heaven,
   hallowed be thy name.
   Thy kingdom come,
   thy will be done on earth as it is in heaven.
Give us this day our daily bread.
And forgive us our trespasses,
   as we forgive those who trespass against us.
And lead us not into temptation,
   but deliver us from evil.
For thine is the kingdom, and the power, and the glory,
   forever. Amen.

From *The United Methodist Hymnal,* #895. Copyright © 1989 The United Methodist Publishing House.

6. SUN MOBILE
THE JOY OF KNOWING GOD

This cheerful mobile represents the joy of knowing God.

BIBLE READING
Romans 15:13

TIME REQUIRED
40 minutes

MATERIALS
large piece of paper

yellow cardstock

gold thread

pencils

scissors

paper punch

gold craft ribbon
(½-inch wide)

glitter glue

black markers

1. Start the lesson by asking "who feels happy today?" Ask the reason for feeling happy. Can they describe what it means to them? Ask the children to think of times when they have felt joy. Start them off with a few suggestions, such as going on vacation, winning a prize, or opening Christmas presents.

2. Explain that these feelings are short-lived and are only temporary happiness. Our joy in knowing God is everlasting. It is a permanent feeling we carry with us for our entire lives. Ask a volunteer to read Romans 15:13 aloud to the class.

3. Draw a simple picture of the sun with a smiling face on a large piece of paper. Explain that this cheerful sun represents the joy we have in knowing God. Invite the children to make a mobile decorated with sunny faces. Remind the children that without the sun we would not exist, just as we would not exist without God.

4. Distribute the materials for the craft. Draw a sketch on the paper of how the mobile should be constructed. Show the children how to draw and cut out four sun shapes from the yellow cardstock—one large and three small ones of equal size. Punch holes to hang the small suns from the large sun with pieces of gold thread. Then tie a piece of gold ribbon to the upper point of the large sun to suspend the mobile from the ceiling. Draw a happy expression on the face of each sun (front and back). Then give them a sparkly effect by decorating both sides with glitter glue.

5. As the children make their mobiles, discuss some of the ways God brings us joy, such as:

- God created us individually, so we know we are special;
- God sent God's Son, Jesus, to show us love;
- God has promised us eternal life;
- God gave us the Bible so we can have happy lives;
- God always listens to our prayers;
- God forgives us and loves us;
- God provides for us;
- We can trust God with our lives.

6. When the children have finished making their mobiles, ask if they can think of other ways we can feel happy. Help them to realize that we can have a deeper happiness by enjoying a close relationship with God, doing things that please God, and telling other people about Jesus.

7. Conclude by asking a volunteer to read the prayer.

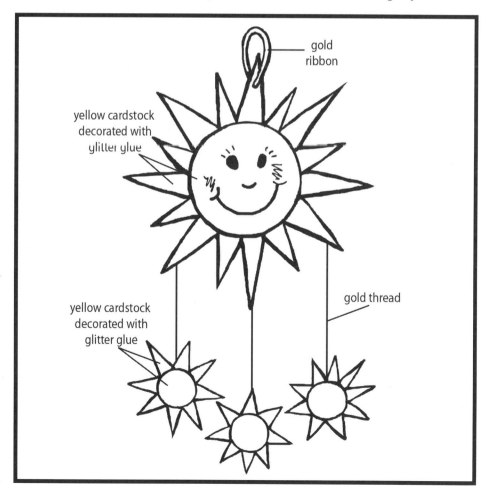

gold ribbon

yellow cardstock decorated with glitter glue

gold thread

yellow cardstock decorated with glitter glue

7. CANDY HEARTS
JESUS' MESSAGE OF LOVE

Children can think about Jesus' love for everyone as they make these sweet hearts.

PREPARATION

To prepare the candy hearts mixture, sift the confectioner's sugar. Beat the egg whites and gradually stir in the confectioner's sugar. Add a few drops of vanilla extract and red food coloring. Mix until smooth. Form a ball and wrap in plastic wrap. Store in an airtight container at room temperature. The mixture hardens in about two hours when exposed to air or refrigerated. This quantity makes 10-12 hearts.

IMPORTANT

Spread wax paper on a clean surface to make the hearts. Be sure the children's hands are washed.

1. Ask a volunteer to read the Bible passages aloud. Ask the children what the passages tell us about how God wants us to treat each other. Write the key words on a large piece of paper. Explain that Jesus spread a message of love, compassion, kindness, forgiveness, fairness, sincerity, and honesty. He showed love for all of us without judging us in any way. Because we are God's people, we should strive to follow Jesus' example and treat everyone as Jesus did. Ask the children to suggest some specific ways in which we can show love and kindness to others, such as:

caring about people

being friends with those who are not popular

being honest and fair

helping friends and family

showing compassion

being tolerant and forgiving

BIBLE READING

Colossians 3:12-14
and John 15:12

TIME REQUIRED

40 minutes

MATERIALS

confectioner's sugar
(1 lb for recipe plus small
amount in bowl)

2 egg whites

vanilla extract

red food coloring

plastic wrap

airtight container

wax paper

rolling pins

heart-shaped cookie cutters

plastic knives

paper plates

large piece of paper

marker

Draw a simple heart on the paper. Explain that the heart is a symbol of love. Invite the children to make candy hearts to take home and share with family and friends.

2. Give each child a lump of the mixture on a piece of wax paper. Put the rolling pins, plastic knives, cookie cutters, and a bowl of confectioner's sugar where they can be easily reached. Show the children how to coat their hands, rolling pin, and cookie cutters lightly with confectioner's sugar to keep the mixture from sticking, and then roll out the mixture to half an inch thickness. Cut out the hearts with the cookie cutters. Use a plastic knife to lift the hearts carefully onto the paper plates.

3. As the children make their candy hearts, discuss some of the ways Jesus showed his love for people. He healed the sick and disabled, fed the hungry, befriended the unpopular, and taught people to love each other. Ask the children to think of more examples.

4. When the children have finished their candy hearts, ask a volunteer to read the prayer. Encourage the children to spend some time every day reflecting on how Jesus demonstrated his love for everyone. Encourage them to think of ways they can follow his example.

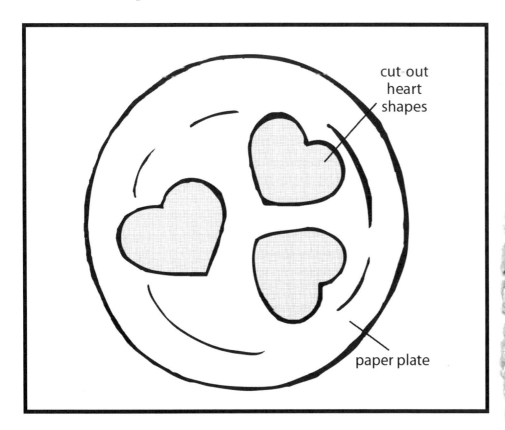

cut-out heart shapes

paper plate

PRAYER
Dear Jesus, thank you for teaching us to love one another. Please help us to follow your example. Amen.

8.

PLACE MAT
THE FRUIT OF THE SPIRIT

Making these printed place mats will help children recognize the fruit of the spirit within themselves.

BIBLE READING
Galatians 5:22-23

TIME REQUIRED
45 minutes

MATERIALS

natural fabric
(such as burlap
in light colors)

knife
(for teacher's use)

dissolved flavored gelatin
(assorted colors)

clean, new paintbrushes

paper towels

selection of fruits and vegetables, suitable for stamping, e.g. carrots, apples, bell peppers, bananas and oranges

large piece of paper

PREPARATION

Cut light-colored natural fabric (such as burlap) into 14- by 12-inch rectangles, one per child. Dissolve different flavors of gelatin in boiling water. Note: use half the recommended water so that the liquid will be thick.

1. Choose a volunteer to read Galatians 5:22-23 to the class. Then ask the children if they understand what the Holy Spirit is. Explain that when we accept Jesus as our Savior and give our lives to God, God sends the Holy Spirit into our hearts to help us develop a godly character. This means that God's qualities are growing constantly within us and become part of our personality. The Bible passage tells us what these qualities are. List them on a large piece of paper: love, joy, peace, patience, kindness, generosity, faithfulness, gentleness, and self-control.

2. Cut open an apple and show the children the seeds in the core. Explain that as we grow in faith, learning more about God, praying regularly, and studying the Bible, the Spirit within us will develop from a seed and bear fruit.

3. Cut the fruit and vegetables in half and show the children how to make stamped prints on their place mats. Spread a little of the dissolved gelatin liquid evenly on the flat side of the fruits and vegetables, then carefully press each one down on the fabric. Only press once or the color will smudge. Pat the surface dry gently with a piece of paper towel. Allow the children to make the fruit and vegetable patterns of their choice.

4. When the place mats are completed, set them aside to dry. Read the Bible passage to the children again and focus on the meaning of these qualities:

- Love means to care unconditionally about others;
- Joy is feeling happy because we know God cares for us;
- Peace comes from feeling content because we have God in our lives;
- Patience is being tolerant of others, despite their behavior or character;
- Kindness involves helping, sharing, and showing concern and compassion, just as Jesus did;
- Generosity is not only the willingness to give; it is to give completely without putting our own wants or needs first;
- Faithfulness is believing and trusting in God completely, no matter how we may be challenged and tested;
- Gentleness is being humble, mild and modest;
- Self-control means to be a model of good behavior and thinking before acting.

Remind the children that these are the qualities God wants us to develop. Invite the children to rinse the fruits and vegetables that they used for the prints and to enjoy them as a snack. Conclude with the prayer.

PRAYER
Loving God, help us to become more like you by sending your Spirit into our hearts. Amen.

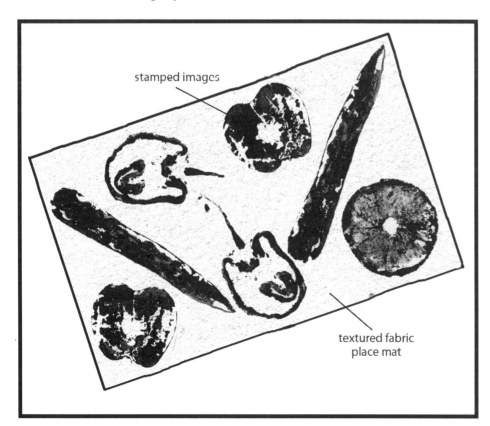

stamped images

textured fabric place mat

9. BOTTLE GARDEN

TRUSTING IN GOD

This garden in a bottle has firm roots, representing the strength of our trust in God.

BIBLE READING

Jeremiah 17:7-8

TIME REQUIRED

40 minutes

MATERIALS

jars with wide openings (one per child)

potting soil (small bag)

seedlings (different varieties, sufficient quantity for each child to have 3-4)

long-handled spoons

acrylic paints (assorted colors)

paintbrushes

PREPARATION

Put a notice on the church notice board or in the newsletter asking for donations of large jars and plant seedlings.

1. Ask a volunteer to read Jeremiah 17:7-8 to the class. Explain that the Bible passage compares trust in God to a tree that has growing roots. When we put our trust in God, we create the roots of faith. These roots grow stronger over time as we learn more about God and develop our friendship with God.

2. We can see in the Bible examples of people who trusted God. Noah obeyed God without question when he was told to build the ark and collect all the animals. It must have seemed an enormous task, but he agreed to do it because he trusted God completely. Daniel knew God would protect him from being killed by lions, and he was saved because of his trust in God. Allow time for the children to read these stories: Genesis 7:1-5, 17; 8:6-12 and Daniel 6:11-23.

3. Explain to the class that they are going to create a garden in a bottle, where they will be able to see the roots of their plants growing. Give everyone a jar in which to grow their bottle garden. Show the children how to put about two inches of potting soil in the bottom of their jar, and press it down gently using a spoon. Distribute the seedlings. Warn the children to handle them carefully as they are fragile. Show them how to dig small holes in the soil with a spoon to plant each individual seedling in their gardens.

4. When the children have finished planting, have them wipe away any dirt from the exterior of their jars with a paper towel. Then give out the paints and brushes for the children to decorate their jars.

5. As the children make their bottle gardens, explain that when we trust God, we can give our lives over to God. We can know that God will always do what is best for us. God is with us everywhere we go. God will help us to make the right choices in all that we do, both now and in the future.

6. When the children have completed their bottle gardens, remind them to put their jars in a sunny position at home and to water their plants regularly, but caution them to use a small amount of water because there are no holes for extra water to drain. Conclude by asking a volunteer to read the prayer.

child's painting

seedlings

soil

25

10. CANDLE HOLDER
THE LIGHT JESUS BRINGS

With this decorated candle holder, children can meditate on Jesus being the light in our lives.

BIBLE READING
John 8:12
Ephesians 5:8-9

TIME REQUIRED
30 minutes

MATERIALS
candles
(one per child plus
one for the teacher)

matches

clean glass jars
(one per child)

acrylic paints
(assorted colors)

paintbrushes

glitter glue,
stick-on gems and
beads, stickers
(to decorate)

PREPARATION

Before the children arrive, turn off the lights and darken the room. Light a candle and place it on a table in the center of the room. Clear sufficient space for the children to gather around it.

1. When the children arrive, ask them to meditate quietly on the candle's flame and think about Jesus for a few minutes.

2. Turn on the lights and extinguish the candle. Ask a volunteer to read the Bible verses aloud. Explain that when Jesus came to the earth, he was like a spiritual light, bringing knowledge of God into the darkness. This is why Jesus is often referred to as "the light of the world." The Bible verses tell us that by following Jesus, we will live in a way that pleases God and brings us happiness.

3. Distribute the craft materials. Explain that the children will make candle holders as a reminder that Jesus is the light in our lives. Using the paints, the children can write "Jesus" on their jars, and then decorate them as they choose with the gems, beads, stickers, glitter glue, and so forth.

4. As they make their candle holders, discuss how we can live in the light of Jesus by

always being honest and trustworthy

being fair in all things

serving others

caring about other people

being a good friend

showing forgiveness
being compassionate
sharing and giving
obeying God
praying regularly
studying the Bible

Ask the children to think of more examples.

5. When everyone has completed a candle holder, darken the room and light the candle on the center table again. Invite the children to stand around the candle and focus on it while you read the prayer.

IMPORTANT NOTE

Give the children's candles to them at the end of the lesson. Tell them that they must not light their candles unless supervised by an adult.

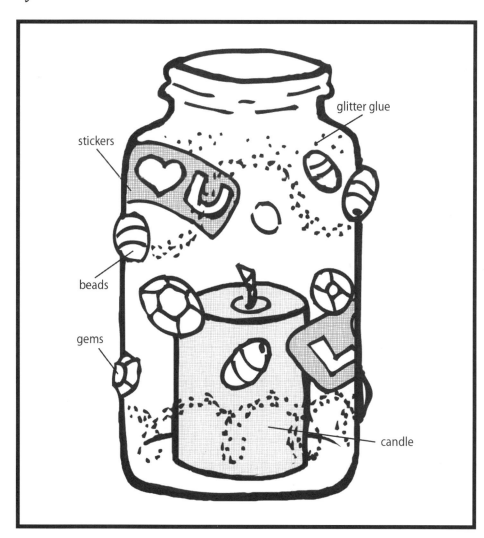

glitter glue

stickers

beads

gems

candle

11. FISHING GAME

BRINGING OTHERS TO JESUS

As they make this fun game, children will learn that bringing others to Jesus will make them "fishers of people."

BIBLE READING

Matthew 28:18-20
Mark 1:16-18

TIME REQUIRED

30-35 minutes

MATERIALS

large piece of paper

unlined index cards
(assorted colors)

small ring-shaped magnets
(1 per child)

paper clips (4 per child)

colored markers

pencils

scissors

string
(one 18-inch piece per
child)

12-inch wooden dowels

1. Start the lesson by asking the children if they talk about Jesus and God with their friends. Explain that God wants us to be friends with everyone. God wants us to tell as many people as possible about our faith. When we do this, it is called "witnessing." This means we bring others to God by sharing our faith.

2. Ask a volunteer to read Matthew 28:18-20 to the class. Explain that when we witness to other people, we are being disciples. The Bible passage tells us that Jesus wants us to make more people into his disciples. Discuss how it can be difficult to talk about Jesus to some of our friends, but assure them that God will help them. Encourage the children to think of Jesus as their best friend; this will make it easier to talk about him.

3. Hand out the pens and paper to everyone. Ask the children to write down the names of people they know who do not attend church. Allow five minutes for this. Add up the total number of people from the lists and write the figure on a large piece of paper. Tell the children that God would be very happy if God could become friends with all these people. Then ask a volunteer to read Mark 1:16-18 aloud. Explain that when Jesus said that he and his disciples would be "fishers of people," he meant that they would tell others about God and catch them like fish. Tell the children that they are going to make a game that involves catching fish. The fish represent people who do not know God.

4. Distribute the pencils, cards, markers, scissors, and paper clips. The children can draw four fish on the cards, cut them out, and draw in features with the colored markers. Show them how to attach a paper clip to the mouth of each fish. The magnets on the fishing rods will attach to these and "catch" the fish. To make the fishing rods, tie a ring-shaped magnet to one end of the string and tie the other end to the dowel.

5. When the children have finished making their games, discuss the following ways to share our faith. We can start by asking family, friends and neighbors to attend church with us. We can tell them how Jesus spread a message of love and showed us how to treat each other. Another way of witnessing is to follow Jesus' example. By being thoughtful, respectful of others, loving and kind, we draw people to us, which provides the opportunity to share our faith.

6. Allow the children to play their fishing games before finishing the lesson with the prayer.

NOTE

Some children may not feel comfortable about witnessing and may not be ready or confident enough until they are older. Make sure they understand the facts before sharing their faith, but encourage them to express their personal feelings too.

PRAYER

Lord, please help us to share our faith and serve as your disciples. Amen.

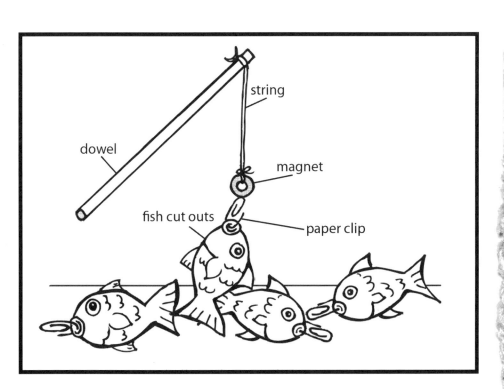

dowel

string

magnet

fish cut outs

paper clip

12. ANIMAL BADGES
CARING FOR GOD'S CREATURES

These eye-catching animal badges will invite discussion about caring for God's creatures.

NOTE

The week before this activity, ask the children to bring photographs of their pets to this lesson.

OPTIONAL

The children can bring their pets to the lesson.

PREPARATION

Cut the felt into 4-inch squares. Use colors such as gray, brown, cream, yellow, and other colors suitable for animals. Use a drinking glass or cookie cutter to draw circles on the felt. Draw circles on the cardstock too. Each child will need one.

1. Ask the children with photographs of their pets to pass them around for everyone to see. Spend a few minutes talking about them. For children without pets, ask them what pet they would like to have. Ask a volunteer to read the Bible verses. Explain that when God created animals, God gave us the responsibility for their well-being. When we take good care of our pets, we are pleasing God. It is important that we take care of all animals, not just our own. The Bible gives us clear instructions about this, as we have seen in the Bible readings.

2. Divide the children into small groups and give them pens and paper. Ask them to think of ways we can look after God's creatures. Allow ten minutes for this, then write down their ideas on a large piece of paper. Be sure to include the following: taking pets to the veterinarian when they are sick,

BIBLE READING

Proverbs 12:10a
Exodus 23:4-5
Psalm 50:10-11

TIME REQUIRED

40 minutes

MATERIALS

large piece of paper

stiff cardstock

felt squares
(2 per child)

scissors

craft glue

large safety pins
(one per child)

fabric markers

scraps of felt
(assorted colors)

hot glue gun

making sure they have food and fresh water, being kind to all animals and never harming them, telling parents if they see a lost pet or if they see someone hurting an animal.

3. Explain that God instructed Noah to save the animals because God cared so much about them. Animals are an important part of God's world, and God expects us to love and respect them and take care of their needs. With this in mind, the children can make badges that resemble the faces of their pets.

4. Invite the children to cut out two felt circles and one card circle for each animal badge. Glue the safety pin in the center of one of the felt circles using the hot glue gun. (Note: use the hot glue gun yourself or carefully supervise older children.) Stick the card circle to the back of this felt circle using craft glue. To make the pet faces, cut out eyes, noses, ears, mouths, and whiskers from the scraps of felt and glue them on the remaining felt circle with craft glue. Use fabric markers to add any extra detail. Glue the completed face onto the card circle.

5. When the children have finished making their badges, suggest they put them on. Tell them that when friends notice their badges, they can explain the significance. Conclude by reading the prayer together. If any children have special requests, such as healing for a sick pet, include these in the prayer.

felt circles and felt scrap pieces

features added with marker

13. WINDOW DECORATION
GOD'S LOVE FOR US

This stained-glass window is an effective reminder of God's love.

1. Before the lesson, draw a simple cross on a large piece of paper. Ask a volunteer to read the Bible verse. Ask the children if they understand the connection between the verse and the symbol of the cross.

2. Explain that the Bible tells us that God showed us what it means to really love through the birth, life, death and resurrection of Jesus. Jesus is the Savior for the world, but Jesus is also the Savior for each of us. That is how much God loves each of us. When we believe in Jesus, we can know with confidence that we are loved now and forever.

3. Point to the cross on the paper and explain that it reminds us of Jesus' life, death, and resurrection. Whenever we see this symbol, we should remember how much God loves us. The children can now make their own crosses to display at home as a reminder. Give each child a piece of wax paper that is slightly larger than your construction paper sheets. Have them tear pieces of various colors of art tissue ranging in size from thumb-sized to palm-sized. Show them how to use diluted white glue to "paint" the art tissue pieces onto the wax paper.

4. Next, the children should use white pencil or chalk to draw the outline of a large cross on a sheet of black construction paper. Have them cut out the shape from the card and discard it, leaving the cross "window" in the card. They can also cut out a decorative border or pattern if they wish. When they have finished cutting, have them glue the covered wax paper to the back of the construction paper and trim to fit. The colors will show through the cut-out spaces, producing a stained-glass window in the shape of a cross.

BIBLE READING
John 3:16

TIME REQUIRED
30 minutes

MATERIALS
large piece of paper

marker

black construction paper (one sheet per child)

wax paper

art tissue (assorted colors)

diluted white glue

paintbrushes

white pencils or chalk

scissors

tape

5. **A**s the children make their window decorations, discuss how they can show their gratitude to God by

finding out more about God

developing a real friendship with God

worshiping God and giving thanks for Jesus

believing in Jesus and following his teaching

Ask the children for their own suggestions.

6. **W**hen the crosses are complete, tape them to a window. Gather the children around the window and pray together.

PRAYER
Dear God, Thank you for loving us so much that you would send your Son to prove your love for us. Amen.

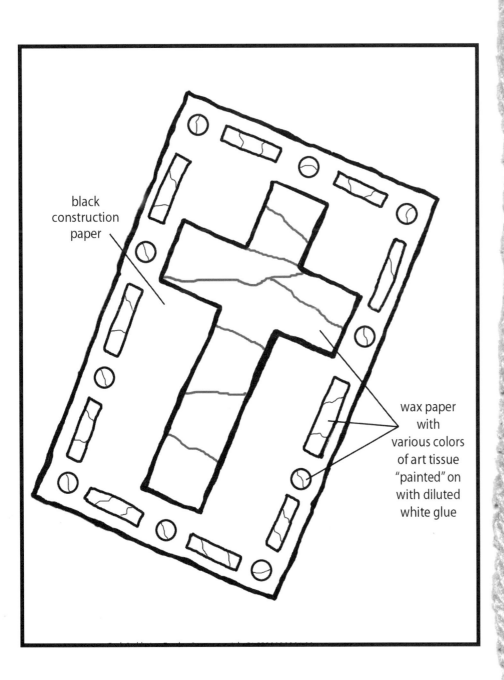

black construction paper

wax paper with various colors of art tissue "painted" on with diluted white glue

14. CLASS COLLAGE
GOD'S KINGDOM

Children can work together on this collage that expresses their thoughts about God's kingdom.

PREPARATION

Use the church newsletter to request donations of magazines. Check the content of them prior to the lesson and remove any unsuitable material.

1. Before the children arrive, copy the following Bible references onto a large piece of paper: Micah 4:3, Isaiah 11:6-8, 35:5-6, 65:21-24, and Psalm 37:29.

2. Choose a volunteer to read Philippians 3:20 and John 14:2 to the class. Explain that both passages refer to God's kingdom of heaven. Ask the children how they picture heaven in their minds. Explain that the Bible gives us some information about what we can expect.

3. Ask the children to look up the Bible references on the paper. Discuss them individually

- In God's kingdom, everyone will live in peace. There will be no war or weapons (Micah 4:3).
- All creatures will live in harmony. Even wolves and sheep will live together. Little children will take care of them (Isaiah 11:6-8).
- No one will be sick, and all disabilities will be cured (Isaiah 35:5-6).
- There will be food and housing for everyone. All our prayers will be answered (Isaiah 65:21-24).
- Only good people will be in God's kingdom, so there will be no crime or violence (Psalm 37:29).

BIBLE READING
Philippians 3:20
John 14:2

TIME REQUIRED
45 minutes

MATERIALS
large piece of paper

posterboard

glue sticks

scissors

diluted white glue

paintbrushes

stapler / staples

magazines

4. **D**istribute the craft materials and magazines. Using pictures from the magazines combined with their own drawings, the children can create a collage that shows their view of God's kingdom. Remind them to use the knowledge they have from the Bible. If the children need help, suggest pictures of people smiling, spacious homes, children playing, beautiful scenery, and so forth. Encourage all the children to add their own personal touches too. Instruct the children to cut out pictures from the magazines and glue them on the posterboard until the posterboard is completely covered. If you have a large class and you are having the children work on several collages, the sheets of posterboard can be stapled together to create a giant poster. Distribute the paintbrushes and diluted white glue for the children to paint over the entire surface of the poster. This gives it a shiny appearance when dry.

5. **G**ather everyone around the collage. Invite the children to reflect on God's promise of heaven for a few moments. Ask a volunteer to read the prayer.

PRAYER

Almighty God, thank you for your promise of heaven to all of us who are faithful to you.
Amen.

15. PIGGY BANK
CHARITABLE GIVING

This piggy bank is a reminder that charitable giving helps others and pleases God.

1. Ask the children how they feel when they receive a gift (probably excited, pleased, and grateful). Then ask how they feel when they give someone a gift. Does it give them a good feeling and make them feel warm inside? Ask which they like best, giving or receiving.

2. Read Acts 20:35 aloud. Tell the children that this clearly shows we will find more happiness in giving than receiving. Discuss giving to charity and ask if their families donate money regularly to the church, charities or other good causes. Explain that God wants us to help needy people through charitable giving. God wants us to do this gladly, not out of duty or reluctantly. Ask who receives an allowance or earns money. What do they spend it on? Do they save any? Can they spare some of that money for the needy?

3. Explain that because God is generous to us, we are able to give to those who need our help. We can give money, but we can also give in other ways, such as helping a friend with homework or gardening for a disabled neighbor. Ask the children to think of ways they can help others.

4. Distribute the craft materials and invite the children to make a piggy bank for their spare coins, to give to the charity of their choice. Mix a few drops of white glue with the paint for the children to paint the bottles pink, or black and white if they prefer, to make the pig's body. They can paint in eyes and the mouth, and paint the bottle cap to resemble a snout. Show them how to cut out ears and a tail from the posterboard. You will need to hot glue them on for the children. Hot glue the corks for each child and stick them to the body as legs, making

BIBLE READING
Acts 20:35
2 Corinthians 9:7-9

TIME REQUIRED
45 minutes

MATERIALS

opaque plastic bottles, such as from bleach or liquid starch, washed and dried (one per child)

acrylic paints (pink, black and white)

white glue

corks (4 per child)

paintbrushes

scissors

white posterboard

masking tape

hot glue gun and craft knife (for teacher's use)

sure that the pig will stand upright and balanced. Use the craft knife to cut a slot in the top of each pig's body for coins to go in. (Caution: use the knife yourself and keep it out of the reach of the children.)

5. As the children make their piggy banks, read aloud 2 Corinthians 9:7-9. Discuss the following aspects of the Bible passage:
• Our giving should be done unselfishly.
• God loves people who give gladly to help others.
• God gives us more than we need so that we can share.

6. When the children have completed their piggy banks, talk with them about possible charities to which to donate their money. Give them a few suggestions, such as overseas missions that distribute Bibles or aid agencies who provide medical help in remote parts of the world. Remind the children that giving money to charity pleases God; but God is equally pleased when we give our time, share what we have, and do kind deeds for others. Ask a volunteer to read the prayer.

front view of piggy bank

coins

cut-out ears

cut-out tail

coin slot

painted snout

Paint piggy bank pink or black and white. Also paint eyes and mouth.

cork legs

16. WALL HANGING
THE LIFE OF JESUS

The life of Jesus can be celebrated in these wall hangings made from fabric.

BIBLE READING
John 6:38-40

TIME REQUIRED
50-60 minutes

MATERIALS

large pieces of calico or similar cotton fabric

pinking shears

craft glue

fabric scraps
(all colors)

scissors

pens

colored markers

large piece of paper

PREPARATION

Put a request in your church newsletter for fabric scraps to insure a good supply for this activity. Cut the large pieces of fabric into rectangles measuring 30- by 18-inches. You will need one per child. Ask for a volunteer to hem them or cut them to size with pinking shears to prevent fraying.

NOTE

To minimize mess, put all the tables together, with chairs around the outside. Put the fabric, scissors, glue, and other materials in the middle.

1. Read the Bible passage aloud and explain to the children that they will focus on Jesus' life. The craft will be a series of wall hangings that depict some of the significant events in his life.

2. Briefly discuss some of the events in Jesus' life. Make a list on a large piece of paper: The birth of Jesus, Jesus being baptized by John the Baptist, Jesus healing the sick, Jesus feeding the five thousand, Jesus calming the storm, Jesus teaching, the Last Supper, the cross, the empty tomb.

3. Ask the children to choose one of these events (encourage them to choose different ones). Invite them to create a picture by cutting the fabric scraps into shapes and gluing them onto the background fabric. They can draw in faces and detail with colored markers. Some children may need help with cutting the fabric. If the class is large, the children can work in pairs. Help the children find the Bible passage describing the events. Encourage the children to read the passage before starting their craft.

4. As the children make their wall hangings, explain that when we study the Bible, we can read about Jesus and understand how God wants us to live, for example:

- Jesus taught people about God and the promise of everlasting life.
- Jesus forgave everyone who was against him.
- Jesus had compassion for people, especially the poor and those rejected by society.
- Jesus showed love, kindness, and mercy to all.

Ask the children to think of more examples.

5. Display the individual wall hangings in order as they are finished. Ask each child to tell the class about his or her craft. Help the children to reflect on the life of Jesus. Ask a volunteer to read the prayer.

PRAYER

Dear Jesus, our Savior, you came to earth to save us all. We thank you for everything you have done for us. Amen.

two ideas for fabric hangings

17. FLOWER POT
GROWING IN FAITH

Children can think about growing in faith as they make this colorful flower pot.

NOTE

This craft uses a simple technique for making papier-mache.

BIBLE READING
Luke 8:5-15

TIME REQUIRED
one hour

MATERIALS

large plastic cups (one per child)

white scrap paper

paintbrushes

white glue

acrylic paints (assorted colors)

flower seeds (6-8 for each child)

potting potting soil

knitting needle

1. Choose a volunteer to read Luke 8:5-8 to the class. Explain that this story is called a parable. It has a hidden meaning. Jesus used parables to teach people about God. Ask the children what they think the parable means. Explain that people are the ground in the story and the seed is God's message. What happens when people hear God's message? The second part of the parable tells us. Ask the children to listen to how Jesus explained the parable. Then have the children think about which type of ground they are.

2. Choose another volunteer to read Luke 8:11-15. Ensure that all the children understand that this parable is about faith. Discuss how we can grow in faith by staying close to God and trying to please God. We can achieve this through church and Sunday school attendance, personal prayer, and worship, and by following Jesus' example for living, studying the Bible and learning more about God. Tell the children that today's craft is a flower pot, planted with seeds that grow, just as our faith grows.

3. Distribute the scrap white paper, white glue and paintbrushes. Show the children how to tear up strips of the white paper and stick them to the cup using diluted white glue, building up layers. It is not necessary to wait for each layer to dry, but it is important to create even layers so that the cups will stand upright without tilting or wobbling. Distribute the paints. Show the children how to mix a few drops of glue with the paint which they can then use to decorate their flower pots. This will give a shiny finish when dry.

4. As the children work on their craft, talk about the meaning of the word "faith." For example, when we go to bed at night, we have faith that the sun will rise the next morning. Or when we plant the seeds in our flower pots, we have faith that they will grow into plants. Although we cannot see or touch God, we know we can have faith in God because the Bible provides evidence of God's existence. Throughout the Bible, there are examples of people who had great faith in God. A well-known example is Moses, who devoted his life to serving God. His strong faith enabled him to undertake the tremendously difficult task of leading the Israelites from Egypt, at God's command. Encourage the children to think about their own faith as they make their flower pots.

5. When everyone has finished, carefully poke a few holes in the bottom of each flower pot with the knitting needle. Fill the pots with potting soil and plant with seeds. Remind the children to water the pots regularly, and to place them in a sunny position at home.

6. Display the words of the prayer, and invite everyone to read it together.

CRAFT VARIATION

Instead of paint, colored paper or patterned wrapping paper can be used. Give the flower pot a final coat of diluted white glue to seal.

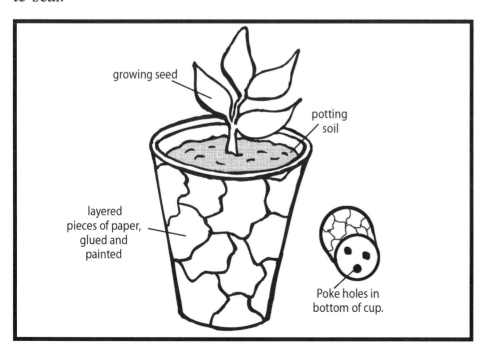

growing seed

potting soil

layered pieces of paper, glued and painted

Poke holes in bottom of cup.

18. PHOTO FRAME
OUR RELATIONSHIP WITH GOD

Making this personalized photo frame encourages the children to think about God and their relationship with God.

NOTE

The children will need to provide a photo of themselves (head and shoulders, if possible) for this craft.

1. Choose a volunteer to read the Bible verses aloud. Affirm that the children are all special to God as individuals and that God loves their different personalities. Explain that by choosing to believe in God and by wanting to know God through prayer, worship, and reading the Bible, we are welcomed into God's family.

2. To reinforce this, the children can make a photo frame to reflect their individuality, their talents, interests, and personal characteristics. Show them how to glue their photo in the center of the black posterboard with glue. Using the crafting foam, they can cut out shapes and glue these around the edges to form a frame. For example, they could cut out the shape of a basketball to represent a talent for sport, a book to show they enjoy reading, or their favorite pet to show a love of animals. Details can be added using the colored markers.

3. As the children make their photo frames, ask them to think about God and their relationship with God. Suggest that they include something on their frame that reflects this. Explain that in order to grow closer to God, we need to be communicating with God and sharing our lives with God.

BIBLE READING
John 1:12
2 Corinthians 6:18

TIME REQUIRED
45 minutes

MATERIALS

black posterboard (one 10-inch square per child)

scraps of crafting foam (assorted colors)

craft glue

scissors

colored markers

pencils

We can have a better relationship with God by

> telling God everything
> being honest with God
> giving thanks and praise
> studying the Bible every day

4. When the children have completed their photo frames, have them sit in a circle facing each other. Ask them to show their photo frames to one another. Encourage them to share something about themselves with the group, perhaps their special interests or future goals. Explain that God is our Father and we are all part of God's spiritual family. Emphasize how important each child is to God.

5. Finish by asking a volunteer to read the prayer.

PRAYER

Father God, we know you love us and see each of us as special. We are happy to be part of your family. Amen.

black posterboard

glued photograph

cut-out images glued on craft foam and glued to frame

19. PENCIL TOPPER
MAKING GOD HAPPY

Children can think about making God happy as they create this smiley face pencil topper.

PREPARATION

Cut the felt into 3-inch squares. Use a drinking glass or cookie cutter to draw circles on the felt squares, ready for the children to cut out. Allow two per child.

1. Choose a volunteer to read the Bible verse to the class. Explain that the Bible tells us that God has feelings. God experiences happiness, just as we do. Ask the children what they think makes God happy. Write their suggestions on a large piece of paper.

2. Explain that making God happy is something we should try to do every day. We can make God happy when we help Mom with the chores when she is tired or when we cheer up a sad friend. Ask the children to think about how we can make God happy. One way is by trying hard to follow Jesus' example. This will spread kindness and love to the people around us. Remind the children that God is always with us.

3. Distribute the craft materials. Tell the children that they can make a smiley face to put on top of a pencil or pen, as a reminder to live as God wants us to live. Show the children how to cut out their two felt circles neatly. Put one on top of the other and glue them together neatly, but only around the edges, leaving a one inch gap to insert the cotton balls. Put pins around the edge to keep in place. (Note: supervise older children or do this for younger ones.) Using the markers, draw in a smiley face. Carefully insert the cotton balls until the face is plumped out, but not over-stuffed. Apply a small amount of glue to the gap, so it is only large enough to fit on a pencil. Pin in place. Tell the children not to remove the pins until the glue is completely dry.

BIBLE READING
Psalm 147:11

TIME REQUIRED
40 minutes

MATERIALS

felt (light colors only)

drinking glass or circle-shaped cookie cutter

scissors

pins

craft glue

colored markers

cotton balls

large piece of paper

needles and colorful thread (optional)

4. As the children make their pencil toppers, discuss the following ways of making God happy: attending church, learning about God in Sunday school, praying regularly, offering our praise and thanksgiving, putting our trust in God, following Jesus, keeping God's Commandments, telling other people about God, reading the Bible.

5. When the children have completed their pencil toppers, encourage them to think about trying to make God happy in everything they do. Ask a volunteer to read the prayer.

NOTE

Have the children leave their pencil toppers in the classroom until they dry. The pins can be removed and discarded once the glue has dried.

CRAFT VARIATION

Instead of using glue and pins to join the felt circles together, older children can sew around the edges with brightly colored thread. Supervise them carefully.

PRAYER

Dear God, we will try our best to make you happy every day. Thank you for the happiness you bring to us. Amen.

20. WIND CHIMES
GOD'S AWESOME POWER

When these seashell chimes blow in the wind, children will be reminded of God's awesome power.

BIBLE READING
Luke 9:42-43

TIME REQUIRED
45 minutes

MATERIALS

pens and paper

large bag of seashells (available from craft stores)

¼-inch dowel (one 5-inch piece per child)

hot glue gun

small bells (4 per child)

narrow ribbon

colored cord

PREPARATION

Cut the narrow ribbon into 14-inch pieces. Allow one per child. Cut the cord into 6-inch pieces. Each child will require four pieces.

1. Ask the children who they think is powerful, such as world leaders, tyrants, rulers of wealthy countries. Explain that humankind has no real power. World leaders may believe they possess power in military strength; tyrants use fear as power; wealthy rulers think they have power in money. When we look at God's power over the world, we can see how truly amazing God is.

2. Choose a volunteer to read the Bible passage. Explain that it tells us how Jesus healed a boy who was possessed by an evil spirit. He did this through God's power. Divide the children into small groups and give them pens and paper. Ask them to think of examples of God's power. They may use their Bibles. Give them the following examples to look up: God's creation of the world, the ten plagues of Egypt, the great flood. Allow five minutes for this.

3. Explain that the greatest proof of God's power is evident in the resurrection of Jesus. Prior to that, God showed God's power through the miracles Jesus performed. Ask the children to turn to the gospels of Matthew, Mark, Luke, and John. Working in their groups, ask them to find as many examples of these miracles as they can. Start them off with Jesus' first miracle in John 2:1-12, where he turned water into wine. Allow fifteen minutes for this.

4. Tell the children that they are going to make wind chimes as a reminder of God's awesome power. We cannot see the wind, but we can see the effect it has just as we can see God's power even though we cannot see God. Distribute the craft materials. Show the children how to glue each end of the ribbon to each end of the dowel, using the glue gun. This will be used to hang the wind chimes. Then glue the four pieces of cord onto the dowel, spaced apart evenly. The shells can now be glued onto the cord. Attach a bell to each end of the four cords to complete the craft. If you have younger children, use the glue gun for them. Supervise older children carefully.

5. Invite the children to hang their wind chimes outside, perhaps near their bedroom window, so they can be reminded of God's power when they hear them ring. Ask a volunteer to read the prayer.

PRAYER
Almighty God, we respect your incredible power and praise your greatness.
Amen.

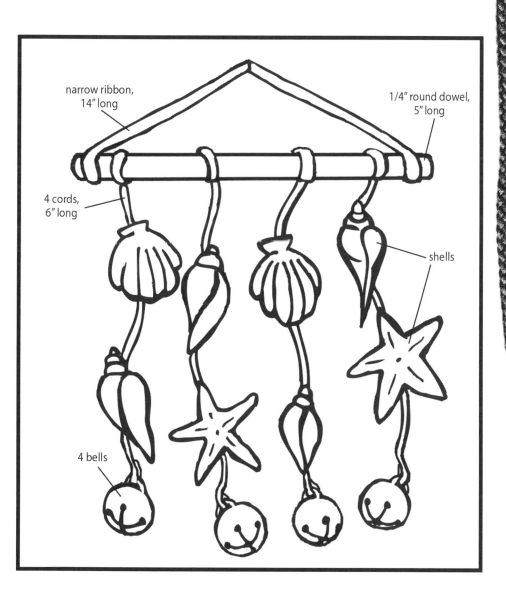

narrow ribbon, 14" long

1/4" round dowel, 5" long

4 cords, 6" long

shells

4 bells

21. MARSHMALLOW CATERPILLAR
NEW LIFE IN JESUS

BIBLE READING
John 3:3
2 Corinthians 5:17

TIME REQUIRED
40 minutes

MATERIALS
pictures of caterpillars and butterflies

large marshmallows (4 per child)

food coloring (assorted colors)

new, fine-tipped paintbrushes

icing mixture (see preparation)

plastic knives

paper plates (one per child)

plastic wrap

colored markers

PREPARATION

You will need to gather pictures of caterpillars and butterflies. Make the icing mixture beforehand by combining confectioner's sugar with water until it has a thick consistency. This will be used as "glue."

1. Read the Bible verses aloud to the class. Explain that the word "Christian" means a follower of Jesus Christ. Ask the children if they have heard the phrase "new life." This means that by becoming a Christian, we leave behind our old lifestyle and start a new life, a new way of living through God. It is as if we start life all over again, by accepting God and receiving Jesus as our Savior.

2. Show the children the pictures of caterpillars and pass them around the class. Ask the children if they know what happens to caterpillars. Show them the pictures of butterflies. Explain that people who become Christians are like caterpillars who turn into butterflies. The caterpillar is gone forever and the butterfly has a new life.

3. Hand out the paper plates and colored markers. Invite the children to decorate their plates with drawings of butterflies, then cover them with plastic wrap. Set the plates aside. The children can now make their marshmallow caterpillars. Show them how to stick the marshmallows together with icing, and then paint them with food coloring.

4. As the children make their caterpillars, discuss how God wants all Christians to help other people get to know God. They can become like butterflies and have a "new life." Christians dedicate their lives to God, making a firm commitment to follow the teachings in the Bible, showing love to one another, witnessing, worshiping God, and following Jesus' example of how to live.

5. When the children have completed their caterpillars, place them on the paper plates, ready to take home. Ask a volunteer to read the prayer.

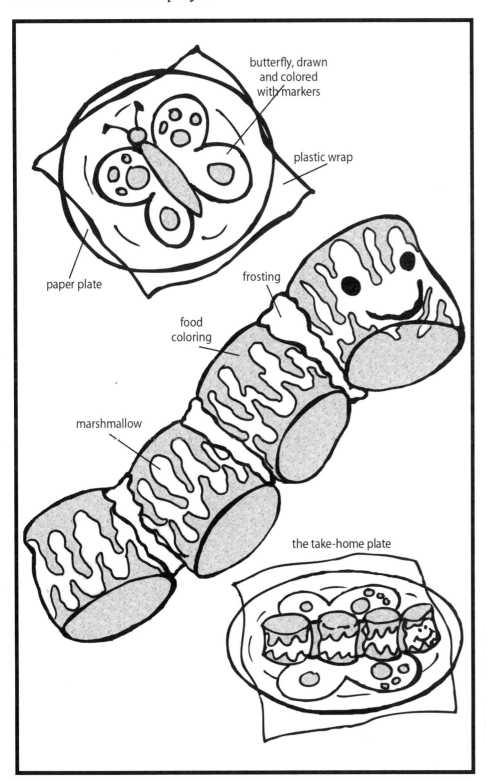

butterfly, drawn and colored with markers

plastic wrap

paper plate

frosting

food coloring

marshmallow

the take-home plate

BIRD FEEDER

TAKING CARE OF GOD'S EARTH

Children can think about the importance of caring for God's earth as they make this bird feeder.

VISUAL AIDS

newspaper, plastic bottle, soda can, glass jar, styrofoam cup

PREPARATION

Photocopy the information sheet (p. 110) for the children to take home with their bird feeders.

1. Place the visual aids on a table where they can be seen clearly. Hold them up, one at a time, and ask the children if they think the following statements are true or false:

a) 500,000 trees are cut down to supply the Sunday newspapers every week.

b) If everyone recycled just one newspaper a week, it would save thirty million trees every year.

c) We use over 2 million plastic bottles every hour.

d) Soda cans can be recycled over and over again.

e) The energy saved from recycling just one can will operate a television for three hours.

f) Every year, we produce enough styrofoam cups to circle the earth 436 times.

g) 28 billion glass bottles and jars are thrown away every year that could be recycled.

2. These statements are all true! Explain to the children that human beings are wasting and using up the earth's resources every day. We must all remember that God created the earth as a gift to humankind, but we do not own our world. The world belongs to God. Read Psalm 24:1 aloud. Explain that God gave us the earth with the responsibility of caring for it. We can all help with this and do simple things to protect God's

BIBLE READING

Genesis 1:27-28
Psalm 24:1

TIME REQUIRED

45 minutes

MATERIALS

milk or juice cartons (one per child), washed and dried

scissors

acrylic paints (dull colors only)

stapler/staples

string (one 18-inch piece per child)

paintbrushes

black sunflower seeds (or wild bird seed)

½-inch dowels (12 inches long) one per child

information sheet (see preparation)

large piece of paper

world. Divide the children into small groups and ask them to think of ways they can save the earth's resources. Make a list on a large piece of paper as they call them out. The list should include recycling, planting trees, conserving forests, and not wasting water.

3. Tell the children that by taking care of the environment, they are showing respect and appreciation for God's great work. We should all do our best to preserve God's world and stop pollution, destruction, and unnecessary waste. This is our duty to God. One way of helping is to provide food for the birds. Read Genesis 1:27-28 aloud. Distribute the craft materials and explain that they are going to help God's world by making a bird feeder.

4. Show the children how to make two small holes opposite each other about one inch from the bottom of the carton using the scissors. This will be to insert the dowel once the feeder is complete, and will serve as a perch for the birds. Cut away the centers of each side, leaving a ½-inch border around the edges and a 2-inch border at the bottom of the carton. The bottom of the carton will be filled with seed later. Staple the top edges of the carton together. The exterior of the carton can now be painted. Use brown and muted green colors that will blend in with the natural surroundings and not frighten the birds away. Staple the string to the top of the carton. This will be used to secure the feeder to a tree branch.

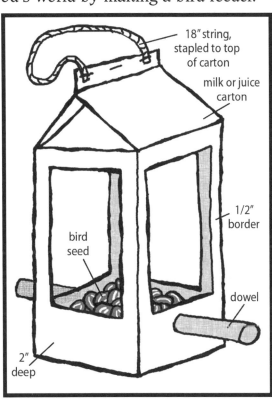

18" string, stapled to top of carton

milk or juice carton

1/2" border

bird seed

dowel

2" deep

5. When the children have completed their bird feeders, fill the base of the carton with seed. Remind the children to hang their bird feeders safely away from cats, and to keep them filled with food regularly. If the weather is suitable, take the class outside and see how many birds they can identify. Ask a volunteer to read the prayer.

NOTE
Give the children the information sheet to take home with their bird feeders.

SEE PAGE 110
for information sheet

PRAYER
Dear God, your world is a special gift to all of us. We promise to help take care of it. Amen.

23. BIBLE BAG

UNDERSTANDING GOD'S MESSAGE

Children can think about God's message as they make this fabric bag to keep their Bible in.

BIBLE READING
2 Timothy 3:16-17

TIME REQUIRED
45 minutes

MATERIALS

felt or cotton fabric

craft glue

pins

scissors

scraps of felt
(assorted colors)

hook and loop fasteners
(one 4-inch strip per child)

needles and sewing thread
(optional)

PREPARATION

Cut the fabric into rectangles measuring 28- by 10-inches and allow one piece per child.

1. Read the Bible passage aloud, asking the children to listen for at least three things it says about the Scriptures. Have them share what they heard. Explain that it is vital to try to learn from the Bible in order to understand God's message. The Bible shows us how to live. There are stories that give us clues about wise ways of living and ways that lead to disaster. Some passages give commands and others give advice. The Bible records the life of Jesus, who is the best example to follow.

2. Tell the children that they can make a bag to keep their Bibles in. Hand out the fabric and show the children how to fold the piece in half (right sides facing outward). Align the edges, and carefully glue the side edges together, leaving the top edge open. Pin the glued edges together. If preferred, the children can sew the seams together, using a running or blanket stitch.

3. Using the fabric scraps, the children can decorate their Bible bags. The bags should be individual and personal to each child, just as his or her relationship with God is. Bags could include the child's name or initials, cut out and glued on the front, and designs such as animals, flowers, abstract shapes, smiley faces, hearts, stars, clouds. To complete the Bible bags, attach the hook and loop fasteners to the top of the inside edges. Remove the pins once the glue has dried. The bags should not be used until the glue is completely dry.

4. As the children make their bags, discuss how God uses the Bible to communicate with us. For example, the Bible

tells us how to build our friendship with God

answers the important questions about life

teaches us about Jesus

gives good advice

tells us how to please God

tells us how to follow God's plan for our future

5. Discuss the best way for the children to learn from their Bibles. Encourage them to read their Bibles every day. Ask a volunteer to read the prayer.

PRAYER

Dear God, guide us and show us what we need to know when we read our Bibles. Amen.

Attach hook and loop fasteners on the inside of the top edge.

Glue side edges together from the top to bottom and pin to secure until dry.

top

sides

sides

bottom

fold of fabric

Alternative Method: Sew instead of glue.

Top

blanket stitch (optional)

Sides

running stitch (optional)

Sides

Bottom

fold of fabric

24. FOOTPRINTS PLAQUE

THE EXAMPLE JESUS SET FOR US

BIBLE READING
2 Peter 1:5-8

TIME REQUIRED
45 minutes

MATERIALS
air-drying clay

plastic plates
(one per child)

rolling pins

acrylic paints
(assorted colors)

paintbrushes

plastic knives

Children can make this wall decoration from clay as a reminder to follow Jesus' example for living.

1. Explain that Jesus showed us how we must live in order to please God. Jesus is the perfect model for us to follow. We need to work hard to make our character like that of Jesus. Explain that by learning about his life we can understand what it means to walk in Jesus' footsteps.

2. Ask the children to think of ways we can follow Jesus' example, such as by

caring about the feelings of others

knowing the Bible well

always being fair

praying regularly

trusting God to help us

being a good friend

sharing our knowledge of God

helping the needy

loving God wholeheartedly

being patient and tolerant

3. Explain that the Bible teaches us how to be like Jesus. Read the Bible passage to the children and ask them to listen carefully as it describes the qualities we need to follow in Jesus' footsteps.

4. Distribute the materials for the craft. The wall plaque is made by rolling the air-drying clay out to ½-inch thickness. Each child will need a piece roughly the size of a tennis ball. This is sufficient to cover a plastic plate. Once the clay is rolled flat, slide a plastic knife under it and carefully manoeuvre it onto the plate. Trim away excess clay using the knife. Smooth any rough edges. Ask the children to remove their socks and shoes. Have each child carefully step on the clay, one foot at a time, to make an imprint of his or her footprints. When they have done this, let everyone paint the clay plaques. Set them aside to dry.

5. When they have finished making the wall plaques, ask the children to reflect on Jesus' qualities for a few moments. Display the prayer and read it aloud with the children.

NOTE

The plaques will take twenty-four hours to dry at room temperature. Once dry, the plates can be removed.

PRAYER

Lord Jesus, thank you for showing us how God wants us to live. Please help us to be like you and follow in your footsteps. Amen.

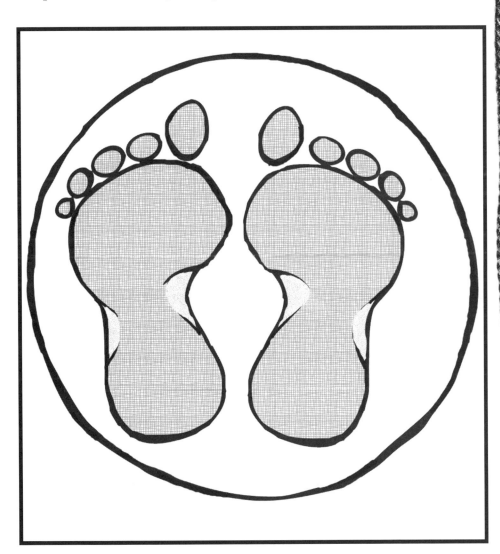

25. MEDAL
SERVING GOD AS OUR GOAL

Children will enjoy making this medal from homemade play dough as they think about serving God.

1. Read the Bible verse aloud to the children. Explain that God wants us to follow Jesus and live a life that pleases God. This can be as challenging as it is for an athlete running a race. When we finish running the race of life, God gives us the prize of everlasting life with God. With this in mind, the children can make an Olympic-style winner's medal, to represent our prize for leading a life that pleases God.

2. Distribute the play dough (a lump the size of a walnut should be sufficient), rolling pins and cutters. Have the children roll their dough out evenly, then press the cookie cutter firmly into the dough to make the medal. Discard the excess dough. Show the children how to smooth the edges of the medal using their fingers.

3. Hand out the wooden skewers, gold paint and paintbrushes. Using the skewers, the children will need to make a hole near the top of their medals to thread with ribbon after baking. Paint the medals with gold paint, then carve a number "1" in the center with the skewer. Add a second coat of gold paint. Carefully place the medals on the baking trays, lined with baking paper. Make sure you have a foolproof way of identifying each medal with its owner.

4. As the children make their medals, discuss what it means to serve God. Explain that in order to serve God, we need to try hard to be like Jesus. Sometimes this may not be easy, but God is always with us, through the Holy Spirit, guiding and helping us to grow as Christians.

BIBLE READING
Philippians 3:14

TIME REQUIRED
40 minutes

MATERIALS

play dough (see recipe)

wooden skewers

rolling pins

round cookie cutters

gold acrylic paint

paintbrushes

baking trays

baking paper

white ribbon (one 36-inch piece per child)

folk art varnish (gloss) or clear wood varnish

Pleasing God should be our goal and we can achieve this by:

- loving God more than anything else;
- finding out about God, knowing God, and talking to God in prayer;
- trusting God completely and relying on God in times of trouble;
- believing that God knows what is best for us;
- following the teachings of Jesus and obeying God's commands;
- using our talents and abilities for pleasing God and fulfilling our purpose in life.

5. When the children have completed their medals, ask everyone in turn to think of one way they can serve God. Choose a volunteer to read the prayer.

6. Bake the medals for nine hours at the lowest possible oven temperature. Varnish both sides and thread with ribbon when dry.

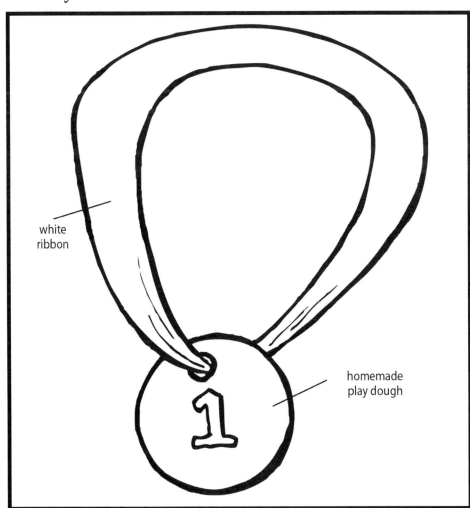

white ribbon

homemade play dough

26. PROMISE KEEPER
GOD'S PROMISES TO US

As the children make this clay pot, they can think about God's promises to God's people.

1. Read the Bible passage to the children. Explain that it refers to God's promise that God would free the people and give them a new land to live in. God kept the promise by choosing Moses to carry out this task. Throughout the Bible we can find many examples of God's promises. Ask the children to look through their Bibles and find some examples. Allow five minutes for this.

2. Explain that God's greatest promise to us is that we can have everlasting life through faith in Jesus. God brought Jesus back to life, giving us proof that God keeps promises. God has promised us many good things, such as:

> to protect us
> to show us mercy
> to love us constantly
> to never desert us
> to forgive us when we do wrong
> to guide us
> to answer our prayers
> to meet our needs
> to provide for us

3. Hand out the craft materials for the children to make their promise keepers. This will be a small coil pot. Show them how to roll out a small piece of clay, approximately 3- by 2-inches, to ¼-inch thick. Use a cookie cutter to cut out the base of the pot. Take small pieces of clay and roll into lengths, so they are shaped like snakes, about ½-inch thick. Lightly moisten the pot base with water and place the first coil on the base,

BIBLE READING
Psalm 106:8-12

TIME REQUIRED
45 minutes

MATERIALS
air-drying clay

rolling pins

plastic knives or modeling tools

round cookie cutters

acrylic paints (assorted colors)

paintbrushes

bowl of water

around the edges. Press down gently. Wet the next coil, and place it on top of the first one. Continue adding coils of wet clay until the pot is about 4 inches high. Try to keep the sides as straight as possible. Using the acrylic paints, use a dark color to paint the inside of the pot. Paint the outside as desired, then leave to dry.

4. As the children make their craft, ask them to think of promises they might like to make to God. Explain that their coil pots are for them to keep their promises in. They can write each individual promise on a piece of paper and put it in their promise keepers. When the children have completed their pots, encourage everyone to think of a promise they can make to God today. For example, they could promise to read their Bibles regularly. Ask a volunteer to read the prayer.

NOTE

The clay pots will take twenty-four hours to dry at room temperature.

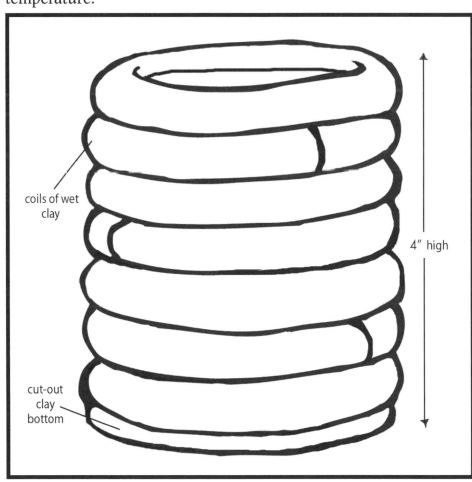

coils of wet clay

4" high

cut-out clay bottom

27. NATIVITY FELTBOARD

CELEBRATE THE BIRTH OF OUR SAVIOR

Celebrate the birth of our Savior with this feltboard that tells the Christmas story.

PREPARATION

Make the feltboards by cutting the thick cardboard into rectangles measuring 18- by 12-inches. Cut the black felt to the same size and glue to the cardboard bases with craft glue. Make one for each child.

1. Have Christmas music playing when the children arrive. Talk about how to many people Christmas is only about gifts and food, instead of about celebrating Jesus' birth. Help the children understand that Christmas is a season of praise and thanksgiving for God's greatest gift—the birth of Jesus. Jesus is the fulfillment of God's promise of a Savior. Ask the children how much they know about the events leading up to Jesus' birth. Read the Bible passage aloud.

2. Show the children the feltboards on which they will create their Nativity scenes to celebrate the birth of Jesus. They can cut simple shapes from scraps of felt to make the stable, the star overhead, Joseph and Mary, Jesus in the manger, the donkey, angel, shepherds, and anything else they choose to add. They can then use the fabric markers to add detail and features. As this is a feltboard, the children can move the pieces around to tell the story of Jesus' birth.

BIBLE READING
Luke 2:4-20

TIME REQUIRED
one hour

MATERIALS
thick cardboard

black felt

felt scraps
(assorted colors)

fabric markers

craft glue

scissors

CD player

CD of Christmas carols

3. **W**hen the children have completed their feltboards, display them and allow time for anyone who wants to tell about their craft. Invite the children to sit quietly for a few minutes and listen to the music as they think about the real meaning of Christmas. Ask a volunteer to read the prayer.

PRAYER

Gracious God, at Christmas we thank you for the wonderful gift of Jesus, our Savior. Amen.

28. DOVE KITE
FINDING PEACE IN JESUS

This flying dove is a symbol of the peace we find in Jesus.

BIBLE READING
John 14:27

TIME REQUIRED
40 minutes

MATERIALS
white posterboard

stapler/staples

paper punch

scissors

glue sticks

white tissue paper

white crepe paper

colored markers

string

dove pattern
(see preparation)

SEE PAGE 111
Dove Pattern

PREPARATION

Photocopy the dove pattern (p. 111), one for each child.

1. Display the dove pattern and tell the children that a white dove is the universal symbol of peace. Ask them what they think it means to be at peace. Not just the absence of war, peace is harmony; peace is the calm and quiet that fills the soul when we have opened our hearts to the work of the Holy Spirit. Jesus urged his followers to be peacemakers.

2. For most people, peace means to feel contented, secure and untroubled. We all have problems and worries throughout our lives, but we can find peace from these by turning to Jesus. Choose a volunteer to read the Bible verse to the class. Explain that these are Jesus' words, telling his followers not to be afraid or troubled. The peace we find in Jesus is something we will not find anywhere else. Some people try to escape their problems and find peace in alcohol, drugs, gambling, and other bad ways of living, but this will not bring them true, lasting peace.

3. Distribute the craft materials and tell the children they are going to make a dove kite that represents the peace we find in Jesus. Show them how to glue the dove pattern to the posterboard. Then they can cut out their kite, carefully following the lines. Show them how to draw in the eyes and color in the beak. Cut long strips of white crepe paper to attach to the tail, 3 or 4 pieces for each dove. These can be secured with staples. Next, show the children how to cut out feather shapes from the tissue paper and glue these to the dove's chest and body. To complete the kite, make a hole near the lower edge of the dove with the paper punch. Thread a long length of string through the hole, making sure it is tied in a secure knot.

4. As the children work on their kites, discuss some of the ways we can find peace whenever we feel upset or afraid. Explain that it can help to read comforting Bible passages or to pray. Jesus is referred to as the "Prince of Peace" in the Bible because he can give us peace with God and peace when we are troubled. Jesus puts our hearts and minds at rest.

5. When the children have completed their kites, take them outside to fly them if the weather allows. As the doves fly high, read the prayer aloud for the children to hear.

PRAYER

Lord Jesus, we know we can find true peace in you. Thank you for always caring about our feelings. Amen.

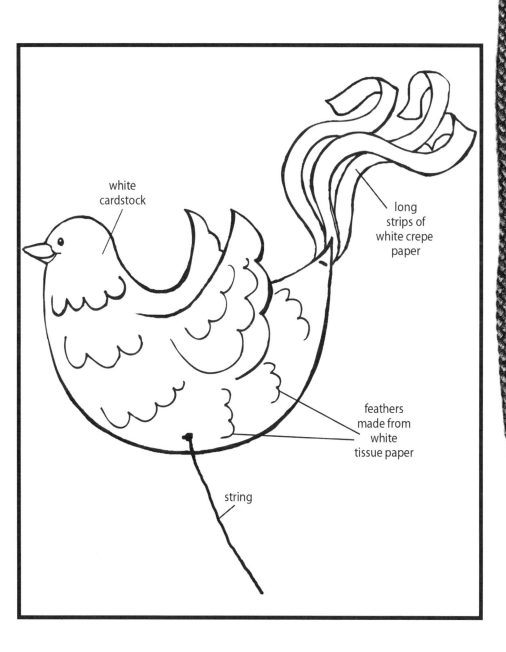

white cardstock

long strips of white crepe paper

feathers made from white tissue paper

string

29. BANNER
RELYING ON GOD

Children can think about relying on God while they make this banner.

PREPARATION

In a bold color, carefully paint the words, "Almighty God, we put ourselves in your hands" across the top of a large light-colored sheet of fabric.

BIBLE READING
Psalm 62:5

TIME REQUIRED
40 minutes

MATERIALS

large piece of paper

paper plates

large piece of fabric for the banner (light colored)

poster paints (assorted colors)

paintbrushes

fabric markers (assorted colors)

thumbtacks, pins, or picture hangers (to hang banner)

1. Read the Bible verse aloud to the children. Explain that we can rely on God to always be close to us; guiding, helping, and watching over us. Read aloud the following:

- God is a friend to the lonely.
- God comforts us when we feel sad.
- God heals our illnesses.
- God listens when we talk.
- God forgives us when we do something wrong.
- God protects us when we are in danger.
- God shares our troubles when we are worried.

2. Ask the children to think about what we rely on God for. Encourage everyone to make a suggestion. Write key words such as love, protection, and comfort on a large piece of paper.

3. Explain that the children are going to make a class banner to hang on the wall as a reminder that we can always rely on God. It will be easier for the children to work on the floor in a spacious area.

4. Lay the sheet of fabric for the banner on the floor and distribute the paints, brushes, and paper plates. Show the children how to coat the plate with their chosen color. Have them press their palm on it, making sure it is completely covered with paint, and then carefully make a handprint on the banner.

5. When each child has made an individual handprint, ask the children to wash their painted hands to avoid mess on the banner. Using the fabric markers, the children can write their names under their own handprints. Then they can add some words of praise to the banner, spread randomly across the fabric. Suggest words such as "God is awesome" or "We love you, God." Leave space on the banner for any class members who are absent.

6. When the banner is complete, hang it on a wall where the children can see it clearly. Gather the class around the banner and pray together.

PRAYER
Awesome God, we know we can rely on you. Thank you for being in our lives and caring for us. Amen.

30. FABRIC PATCHES
CHRISTIAN FRIENDSHIP

These decorated patches display messages of Christian friendship.

PREPARATION

Cut the fabric into 6-inch squares. Allow one per child. Hem the squares or trim the edges with pinking shears to prevent fraying.

1. Choose a volunteer to read Romans 12:10 to the class. Explain that by meeting for Sunday school every week, the children are more than just a class who are there to learn about God. Encourage them to think of each other as brothers and sisters, who are committed to God and to each other in Christian friendship.

2. Divide the class into small groups. Distribute the pens and paper. Explain that having a deep friendship with fellow Christians means caring for each other, just as God cares for us. Ask the children what they think real friendship means. What qualities are important? Working in their groups, ask them to think of at least five qualities they value in friends.

3. Write the following qualities on a large piece of paper: honest, kind, generous, loyal, tolerant, forgiving, encouraging, and supportive. Briefly discuss these and the children's ideas about true friendship. Explain that genuine, loving friendship pleases God and is an extension of our close friendship with God.

4. Move the tables and chairs so that the children are facing each other. If this is not practical, the children can sit in a circle on the floor. Hand out the craft materials and explain that the fabric patches are for their jeans, other clothing, or

BIBLE READING
Romans 12:10
John 13:35

TIME REQUIRED
40 minutes

MATERIALS
cotton fabric
(light colors)
fabric markers
pens and paper
pinking shears
large piece of paper

school bags, and are a personal message of loving friendship from the class. If you have a large class, divide the children into groups of six to seven. Tell each child to use the markers to write their name in the center of their fabric patch. Then have them pass their patches to the person next to them. That child will write a personal message of friendship for the person named on the patch, and then pass it on until everyone has contributed. If time allows, they can make additional patches.

5. While the children are making their patches, read the words of Jesus in John 13:35 to the class. Discuss how we can build friendships that please God. For example, we can pray for each other, show forgiveness, be respectful of each other's feelings, and offer support.

6. When each patch has been returned to its owner, allow the children a few minutes to read the messages. Remind the children that the Bible tells us to think of each other as family members and we must base our Christian friendship on this. Ask a volunteer to read the prayer.

PRAYER
Dear God, we thank you for giving us true friendship between our Christian brothers and sisters. Help us to always be loving and kind to each other. Amen.

67

31. CHOCOLATE BIRD'S NEST

THE EASTER MESSAGE

Children will understand the importance of Easter as they make this edible nest and eggs.

NOTE

This craft requires a microwave oven.

1. Start the lesson by asking the children what Easter means to them. Read the Bible passage to the class, asking them to listen carefully for what it says about God's love for us. Summarize the events leading up to Jesus' resurrection, answering any questions the children might have. Explain that the Resurrection is central to our faith as Christians. Through the Resurrection, God's intention became clear—Jesus is the Christ. Through Jesus, we know God's great love.

2. For Easter, the children can make marzipan eggs in a chocolate nest. Break the cereal up by hand into the bowl. Make sure that there are no large chunks. Add the melted chocolate and mix well. Line the cupcake pans with foil. Show the children how to place a spoonful of the mixture into each space and press the center down with the back of the spoon to form a nest shape. Set aside to harden while the children make the eggs. Give a lump of marzipan to each child. A piece the size of a golf ball is sufficient. From this, they can make small eggs and place them on the paper plates. Show the children how to use the food coloring to paint the eggs carefully. Once the nests are hard, put them on the paper plates and put the marzipan eggs inside.

BIBLE READING
1 John 4:9-10

TIME REQUIRED
45 minutes

MATERIALS

shredded wheat
breakfast cereal

chocolate
(melt in microwave)

spoons

large bowl

aluminum foil

cupcake baking pans
(enough to make a nest for
every child)

marzipan

food coloring
(assorted colors)

fine-tipped paintbrushes

paper plates
(to take nests home)

3. When the children have finished, ask them to sit quietly for a few minutes and silently tell God what Easter means to them. Conclude by reading the prayer together.

CRAFT VARIATION

Use candy or chocolate eggs instead of making them from marzipan. Or decorate one hard-boiled egg per nest.

PRAYER

Loving God, thank you for the new life that is offered to each of us through Jesus. Please bless each one of us. Amen.

foil on baking pan

Use back of spoon to press down middle of each spoonful of nest mixture.

Golf-ball-ized piece of marzipan will make 3 eggs.

marzipan eggs painted with food coloring

eggs in nest on small paper plate

32.

CROWN
OUR BLESSING FROM GOD

This golden crown will help children remember that God strengthens the faithful.

PREPARATION

Give each child a copy of the crown pattern and gold construction paper. Have them use the pattern to cut a crown out of the construction paper. Then ask them to cut out a long strip of construction paper that is about two inches wide. Have them tape one end of the strip to one end of the crown. Fit the crown to each child's head to be certain there is at least a 1-inch overlap.

1. Choose a volunteer to read 2 Samuel 5:10 to the class. Explain that after King Saul died, the people turned to David to be their king. He became the undisputed ruler and united the kingdoms of Israel and Judah into one nation. He selected Jerusalem as his capital city and brought the ark of the covenant to a place of honor in Jerusalem.

2. Ask another volunteer to read 2 Samuel 8:18-28. Explain that David is praying and saying he does not deserve all the wonderful things God has done for him. He praises God and asks God to continue to be with him and bless him. David knows that his strength and success are because of God.

3. Invite the children to decorate their crowns with gems, stars, beads, stickers, and so forth, or draw patterns and shapes with the colored makers. To complete the crowns, bring the ends together and overlap them by one inch. Staple or tape the ends together.

4. When the children have completed their crowns, invite them to wear them. Ask a volunteer to read the prayer to the class.

BIBLE READING
2 Samuel 5:10
2 Samuel 7:18-28, CEV

TIME REQUIRED
30 minutes

MATERIALS
gold construction paper

colored markers

scissors

stapler/staples or tape

sequins, beads, gems, star or heart stickers (to decorate)

glue sticks

PRAYER
Dear God, thank you for our many blessings. Please help us to be strong in our faith. Amen.

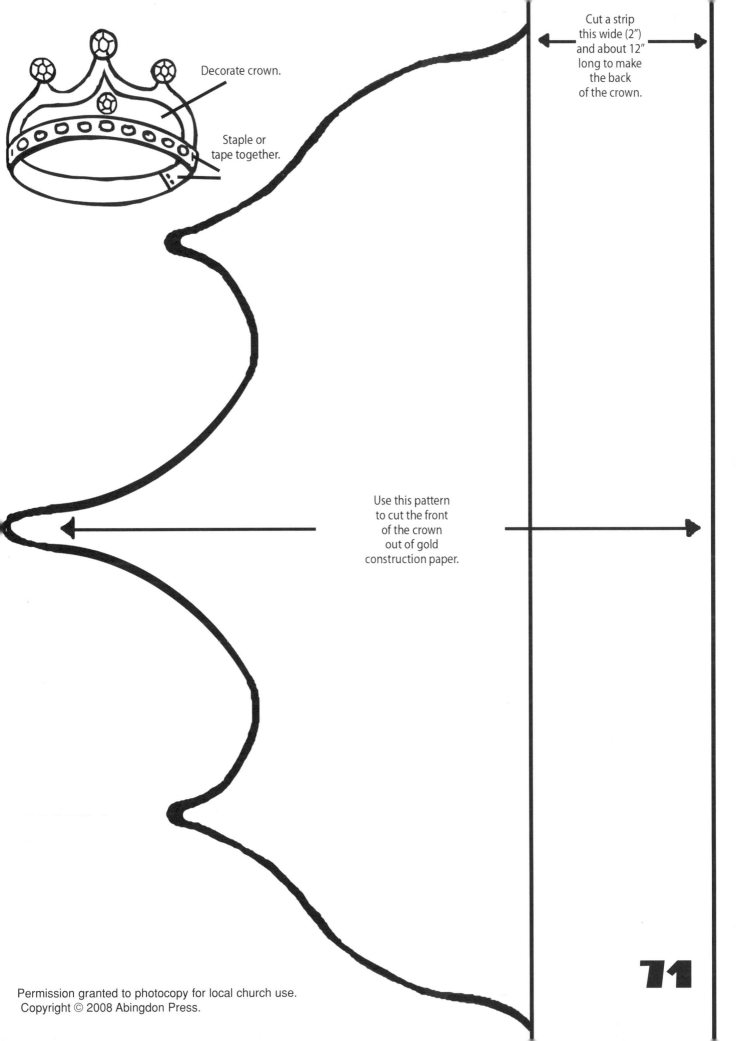

Decorate crown.

Staple or
tape together.

Cut a strip
this wide (2")
and about 12"
long to make
the back
of the crown.

Use this pattern
to cut the front
of the crown
out of gold
construction paper.

71

33. ROSETTE
PUTTING GOD FIRST

Children can think about the importance of putting God first as they make this rosette.

PREPARATION

Cut 2-inch circles from white posterboard. Allow one per child. Cut the ribbon to the required length for each rosette: one 10-inch length of the 2-inch wide ribbon and two 4-inch lengths of the 1-inch wide ribbon.

1. Choose a volunteer to read the Bible verse to the class. Explain that God wants all of us to commit our lives to God. This means putting God first. By doing so, we grow closer to God. To achieve this, we must put aside what we want in order to carry out God's commands. This may sound hard, but it simply means letting God run your life, instead of struggling on your own. By obeying God and following Gods' teaching in the Bible, we can become the people God created us to be.

2. Explain that making a commitment to God does not mean giving up everything we enjoy. Help the children understand that it may involve making some changes in our lives, such as setting aside time just for prayer and Bible study regardless of what else we are doing. It means choosing to do what is right even if we prefer to do something else, for example, staying at home to help mom when she is sick instead of going out with friends.

3. Distribute the craft materials and show the children how to make their rosettes. Take the 10-inch piece of ribbon and glue it carefully around the edge of the card circle with craft glue, pleating it evenly to give a ruffled effect. Trim and glue down the ribbon ends. This is the back of the rosette. Take the two 4-inch pieces of ribbon and glue them on the bottom edge of the back of the rosette in the center, with one slightly overlapping the other. Hot glue the safety pin on the back of the card. (Do this yourself or carefully supervise older children.) Invite the children to write "GOD" on the front with the colored markers and add decorations if they wish.

BIBLE READING
Matthew 22:37

TIME REQUIRED
30 minutes

MATERIALS

reels of satin ribbon (2 inches and 1 inch wide)

white posterboard

craft glue

small safety pins (one per child)

hot glue gun

colored markers

scissors

glitter glue, self-adhesive stars, hearts and gems (optional)

4. As the children make their rosettes, discuss ways they can make a commitment to God. Be certain they include praying regularly, reading the Bible daily, always trying to be like Jesus, and telling others about God.

5. When the rosettes are completed, invite the children to wear them. Explain that when they make the decision to put God first, it is important to tell God. Ask the children to join you in a prayer of commitment.

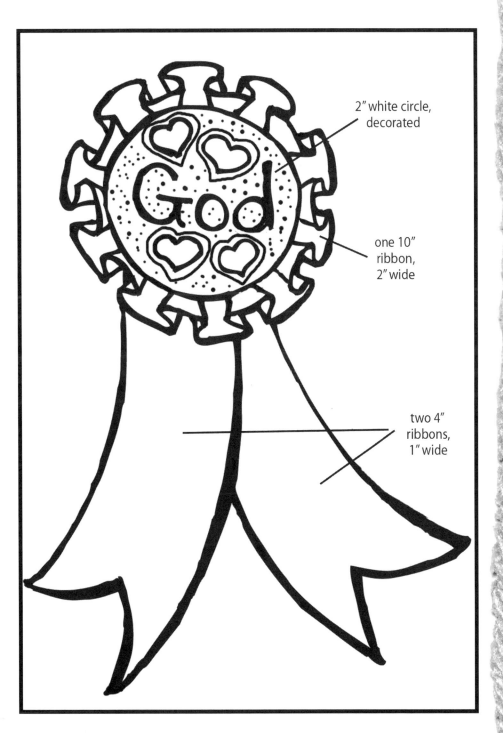

2" white circle, decorated

one 10" ribbon, 2" wide

two 4" ribbons, 1" wide

34. FLAG
PRAISING GOD

As children make this colorful flag, they can think about praising God.

PREPARATION

Cut colored posterboard into 7- by 9- inch rectangles. You will need one for each child.

1. Choose a volunteer to read the Bible verse aloud. Explain that praising God is an important part of our worship. Tell the children that God deserves our praise for so many things, and ask them what they would like to praise God for. Write their responses on a large piece of paper as they call them out.

2. Divide the class into small groups and distribute the pens and paper. Explain that Jesus' ministry brought praise to God. Ask the children to think of ways we can praise God. If they need help, suggest that we can praise God

    in prayer
    by singing songs of worship
    by telling friends about God
    by attending church
    by doing good deeds
    by behaving in a way that pleases God

3. Show the children the materials for the craft. Tell them they are going to make special flags to proclaim God as the Almighty and to praise God for all that God has done for us. Give everyone a posterboard rectangle that will be the flag. Ask the children to write "GOD" in large letters on both sides of the card using the colored markers. Encourage them to decorate their flags with sequins, stars, glitter glue, and stickers. They can also cut out heart and cross shapes from the crafting foam (or use pre-cut foam shapes).

BIBLE READING
1 Chronicles 29:13

TIME REQUIRED
30–40 minutes

MATERIALS
¼-inch dowels (one per child)

colored posterboard

colored markers

glue sticks

scissors

glitter glue, sequins, stickers, self-adhesive stars (to decorate)

pens and paper

hot glue gun

crafting foam

CD player

CD of worship music

large piece of paper

4. As the children make their flags, explain that God does not want us to worship out of duty, but sincerely because of our love for God. We should not just say the words, but praise God honestly from our hearts. When we worship with other believers, we can encourage each other. All sincere worship shows that God comes first in our lives. As the flags are completed, use the hot glue gun to glue them onto the dowels. Do this yourself or carefully supervise older children.

5. When the children are ready, play the music. Encourage them to wave their flags and join in singing praise to God. Be sure to include any shy children. Ask everyone to think of one thing they especially want to praise God for. Ask a volunteer to read the prayer.

PRAYER
Great God, our hearts are full of praise and love for you. We honor you in everything you do. Amen.

7" X 9" posterboard rectangles, decorated

1/4" thick dowel

34. ANGEL SUNCATCHER
GOD'S MESSENGERS

This window decoration is a reminder that we can hear God's message to us.

PREPARATION

Photocopy an angel pattern (p. 112) for each child. Put each pattern copy inside a sheet protector, ready for the children to use.

1. **A**sk three volunteers to read the Scripture passages from the Book of Luke. Explain that there are many stories of angels in the Bible. Tell the children that these heavenly beings are God's messengers.

2. **A**sk the children if they believe in angels. Allow time for them to discuss freely. This craft will remind children that God sends us messages in different ways.

3. **G**ive each child a sheet protector with a copy of the angel pattern inside. Invite them to make an angel suncatcher to display in a window. Place the paint mixtures where they can be easily shared. Show the children how to use the black paint to outline the angel's body, head, hair, wings, robes, and hands. Encourage them to use the other colors to fill in the spaces until the angel is completely colored in with paint.

4. **C**hildren who finish their craft quickly could see what they can discover about angels visiting people from these verses:
Matthew 28:1-4

Acts 5:17-21

Acts 27:23-24

1 Kings: 19:5-8

BIBLE READING

Luke 1:13-14

Luke 1:26-33

Luke 2:10-14

TIME REQUIRED

40 minutes

MATERIALS

angel pattern
(one per child)

plastic sheet protectors
(one per child)

paint mixture
(combine ¼ cup white glue
and ¼ cup liquid tempera in
black, gold, and silver)

tape

SEE PAGE 112
Angel Pattern

5. **W**hen everyone has finished, carefully tape the sheet protectors to a window. Help the children understand that angels are messengers from God. God also speaks to us through Scripture and prayer. Gather the children around the window and pray together.

NOTE

The plastic sheet protectors will need six hours to dry fully. The angels can then be peeled off and stuck to any glass surface.

PRAYER

Loving God, we want to be open to hear your message. Be with us as we read the Bible and as we pray. Amen.

child's painting from pattern on plastic sheet protector

angel pattern inside protector

plastic sheet protector

36. T-SHIRT LOGO
FOLLOWING JESUS

Designing and decorating this t-shirt is a fun craft that will promote thinking and discussion about following Jesus.

BIBLE READING
John 12:26

TIME REQUIRED
45 minutes

MATERIALS

plain white
or light colored t-shirts
(brought by the children
from home)

permanent markers
(in several colors)

paper and pens

large piece of paper

newspaper

PREPARATION

Send a note home with the children one week before you plan to carry out this activity, asking them to bring a plain white or light colored t-shirt. Have some extras on hand for those who don't bring one.

1. Choose a volunteer to read the Bible verse aloud. Explain that Jesus taught people how God wants them to live. Jesus had a special group of followers who were known as his disciples. They went with Jesus from town to town, preaching to people about God and urging others to join them. Jesus told his disciples to spread his message to the whole world. When we encourage other people to follow Jesus, we are being disciples also.

2. Tell the children that they can write a message on a t-shirt to encourage others to follow Jesus. Have the pens, paper, and the permanent markers where the children can share them. Invite each child to design a logo for the front of the t-shirt. Suggest they keep it simple, such as a cross or an outline of the Bible so that it stands out. They can practice their artwork on paper first. Give each child several sheets of newspaper. Show them how to lay their t-shirts flat with the newspapers between the layers of fabric. Warn them to keep the markers away from their clothes.

3. On the back of each t-shirt, the children should write a message, such as:
  • Feeling lost? Follow Jesus.
  • Jesus leads. I follow.

- Who do you follow? Choose Jesus.
- Jesus shows the way. Follow him.

Encourage the children to think of their own slogan. Allow five minutes to draw up a list of suggestions. Write them on a large piece of paper so that the children have the correct spelling.

4. As the children work, ask them to think about Jesus' life and the example he set for his followers. Jesus taught them to be obedient to God, to forgive others, to resist temptation, to serve others, to pray constantly, to show love and kindness to everyone, and to tell people about God's love for all persons and how they can have everlasting life.

5. When the children have completed their designs, invite them to display their t-shirts for the class to see. When the markers are completely dry, let the children put their t-shirts on if they wish. Ask a volunteer to read the prayer.

NOTE

Tell the children and their parents to put the t-shirts in a mixture of vinegar and water before washing for the first time. This will prevent the color from washing away or smearing.

PRAYER
Lord Jesus, please help us to follow you every day and encourage others to do the same.
Amen.

37. FRIDGE MAGNETS

THE IMPORTANCE OF PRAYER

BIBLE READING
Philippians 4:6
Psalm 86:5

TIME REQUIRED
30 minutes

MATERIALS
magnet sheets
(cut into 1-inch squares)
glue sticks
colored, unlined index cards
clear contact paper
colored markers
scissors
large piece of paper

These quick and easy refrigerator magnets provide an important reminder to pray every day.

1. Choose two volunteers to read the Bible verses to the class. Explain that prayer is talking to God and listening to God. When we pray, it is like being with our best friend—one that we love and trust. Prayer is spending time with God and being in personal relationship with God. God hears all our prayers and will answer us in the best way possible, even if the way is different from our request. We can trust God because God is trustworthy and faithful. We must always remember that in God's infinite wisdom, God's will for us is the best answer to our prayers.

2. The children can make a refrigerator magnet with a slogan to remind them to pray regularly. Ask them to think of some suitable slogans that will remind them to pray. Write some suggestions on a large piece of paper to get them started:

• Have you prayed today?

• Talk to God. God listens.

• Looking for answers? Ask God.

The children can choose one of these, but encourage them to make up their own slogan.

3. Distribute the colored, unlined index cards, glue sticks, markers, and magnets. Invite the children to write their slogans on the cards. Show them how to cut the cards into the shape they want, and cover the front with clear contact paper. Glue the magnet on the back. Some children may need help applying the contact paper.

4. **W**hen everyone has finished, talk about the best ways to pray. Suggest they find somewhere quiet where they can relax and talk with God privately. Let the children know that they can take their worries to God and trust God to help. Explain that prayer is also the time to:

• confess sins and ask for God's forgiveness;

• give praise and thanks for what God has done for us;

• ask for peace, courage, protection, purpose, guidance and encouragement;

• pray for others.

Remind the children that prayers should always be honest and sincere. Conclude by reading the prayer together.

38. JIGSAW
THE TEN COMMANDMENTS

Making this jigsaw puzzle will help children to remember God's rules for living.

1. Choose a volunteer to read the Bible passage to everyone. Explain that the Ten Commandments are the holy laws God gave the people to follow thousands of years ago. God wanted us to live the right way, so God gave us the Commandments to help us. Keeping the Commandments shows that we want to be God's people. The Ten Commandments teach us how to love God and one another.

2. Read each Commandment from the Bible, one at a time. Ask the children what they think each Commandment means. Help them to understand these meanings:

1. Put God first. God gives us everything and deserves our worship.
2. We love God and do not want or need false gods.
3. We must always say God's name with respect.
4. God created our world in six days. On the seventh day, God rested. We make this a holy day by attending church.
5. Our parents must be obeyed and respected.
6. God created all life, so it is precious and should not be taken by human hand.
7. Married people must not break their vows of commitment.
8. We should not steal because God provides for us.
9. Always tell the truth. Telling lies can harm the lives of other people.
10. God wants us to be content with what we have and not be jealous or greedy.

3. Distribute the posterboard, colored markers, and scissors for the children to make a jigsaw puzzle. Show them how to cut the posterboard into the shape of a stone tablet. Read the Ten Commandments one at time, and invite the children to write on the tablet the Commandments in their own words. Suggest

BIBLE READING
Exodus 20:1-17

TIME REQUIRED
40 minutes

MATERIALS
colored posterboard

scissors

colored markers

small bags to take puzzle home

craft knife (optional)

they add borders or decorate the tablets. Challenge the children to remember at least three of the Commandments by the end of the lesson.

4. As each person finishes, he or she can cut the posterboard into twenty, even-sized pieces to produce a jigsaw puzzle. Have them mix the pieces up and give them to another class member to put the puzzle together. When everyone has finished, give each child a bag to put his or her pieces in to take home.

5. Ask the children to tell you the Commandments they remember. Encourage them to learn all ten. Ask a volunteer to read the prayer.

TIP
A craft knife makes it easier to cut through posterboard. Cut the children's jigsaw puzzles for them, and keep the craft knife out of reach when it is not being used.

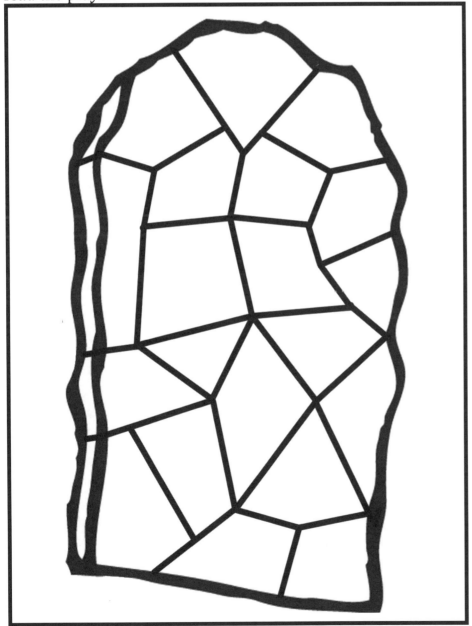

39. GOD'S EYE
THE STRENGTH GOD GIVES US

Children will enjoy making a "God's Eye" as they think about how God gives us strength to do difficult things.

BIBLE READING
1 Samuel 17:45, 48-49

TIME REQUIRED
30 minutes

MATERIALS

craft sticks
(two per child)

scissors

chenille stems

yarn

1. Ask a volunteer to read the Scripture.

2. Explain to the children that the Philistines were a fierce fighting force, one of the Sea Peoples whose land bordered the Great Sea. They wanted the land of Israel, and fought many battles to get control of it. Goliath was one of their most intimidating weapons. Goliath was not the giant that we think of from fairy tales, but he was a really large man—six cubits and a span tall (close to nine and a half feet). In contrast, David was still a young man, too young to even be in King Saul's army at all. David was sent to bring supplies to the army and discover how his older brothers were doing. When he saw how Goliath taunted the army of God, he volunteered to face Goliath armed only with his sling and five smooth stones. God would help him just as in the past.

3. Ask the children who was watching over David and protecting him from Goliath? *(God)* Who is watching over us too? *(God)* Who gave David the strength to defeat Goliath? *(God)* Invite the children to make a "God's Eye" as a reminder that God is always watching over us just like David. God gives us the strength to do difficult things.

4. Give each child two craft sticks of equal length and a chenille stem. Show the children how to arrange the two sticks so that they form a cross. Help the children fasten the sticks together by winding the chenille wire around them. Give each child a length of yarn. (You may need to help each child get started by tying a knot on one of the arms.) Show the children how to begin wrapping yarn at the center of the cross and go around and under each arm. Continue wrapping the yarn in the same direction. Guide the children by repeating, "Around and under, around and under." This will eventually build the yarn from the center to the outer edges of the arms. The portions between the arms should be also covered by the yarn that is going from one arm to the next. When the children have completed wrapping the yarn, help them tie a knot fastening the yarn, leaving a tail of yarn for the children to hang the "God's Eyes" in their rooms at home.

5. When everyone has finished a God's Eye, ask the children to tell you when God has helped them to do something difficult. If they need help, suggest times such as when they were confronted a bully, a time when they were alone and frightened, or a time when they were worried about something new they had to do. Ask a volunteer to read the prayer.

PRAYER
Dear God, just like David, we know you will give us the strength do great things for you. We are happy that you love us no matter what and that you will always watch over us. Amen.

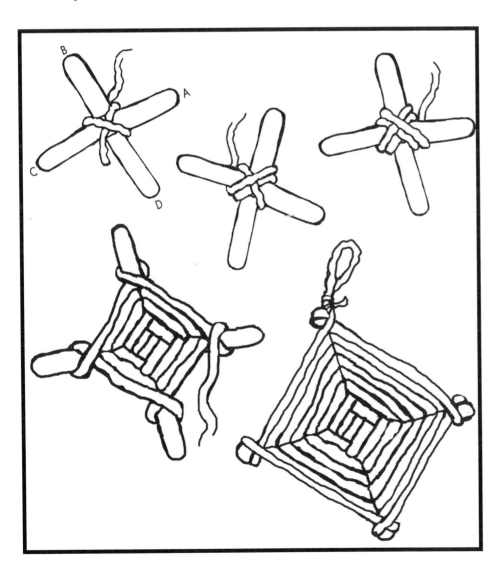

40. PAPER PATCHWORK
GOD'S CREATION

This craft will remind children that God created a wonderful world for us.

BIBLE READING
Psalm 104:5-26

TIME REQUIRED
40 minutes

MATERIALS

white construction paper (one sheet per child)

colored paper (assorted colors)

colored markers

glue sticks

scissors

pencils

pens and paper

PREPARATION

Use a thick, black marker to draw lines on white construction paper, dividing it into six squares. The paper should resemble a patchwork quilt.

1. Read the Bible passage aloud to the children. Explain that Psalm 104 was written in praise of God's creation of the world. Help the children understand that God planned for the earth to be a paradise for God's people, filled with natural wonders and amazing creatures. Divide the class into groups of three or four children, and distribute the pens and paper. Tell the children that we can see examples of God's creation everywhere. Challenge them to think of as many as possible in five minutes and write them on the paper.

2. Ask the children to find Genesis 1:9-31 and read the passage to themselves. Explain that it describes how God made the earth and everything on it.

3. Give out the craft materials for the children to make their paper patchwork quilts. Explain that their patchwork will represent the six days of creation. The patchwork is to be made by cutting paper into the shapes they need. Details can be added by using the markers.

• Using the colored paper, the children can draw the outline of the earth in blue, cut it out, and glue it in the first square on the paper. Then they can cut out countries and glue them onto the earth.

• Continue with a plant for the second day.

• Add a sea creature, such as a fish or dolphin, for the third day.

- Add a bird for the fourth day.
- Add an animal for the fifth day.
- Add a human for the sixth day.

4. As the children make their paper quilts, talk about the truly marvelous earth God made for us, with 4,000 different kinds of plants, 25,000 kinds of fish, 9,000 kinds of birds, and over 4,600 different mammal species.

5. When the children have completed their paper quilts, ask them which of God's creations they like most. Ask a volunteer to read the prayer.

PRAYER
Creator God, thank you for giving us our beautiful world with all its wonders to enjoy. Amen.

41. HARVEST WREATH
GOD'S PROVISION FOR US

Children can think about how God provides for us as they make this harvest wreath.

PREPARATION

Prepare the wreath bases from thick cardboard. Use a dinner plate to make the outer circle the correct size, then cut an inner circle using a smaller plate. Cut out and discard the inner circle so that you have a cardboard hoop.

1. Choose a volunteer to read the Bible verses to the class. Explain that after God created the world, God planned to provide for humankind and all the creatures God had made. To do this, God supplied the earth with over 400,000 different kinds of plants, so humans and animals would have the type of food and shelter they need. Explain that plants produce so much fruit and seed that people can harvest them for food.

2. Distribute the seed pods, pine cones, and other natural materials. Pull apart some of the seed pods and be enthusiastic about how many seeds a tree can produce every year. Marvel at the way a huge tree started out as a tiny seed. Show the children how to make a harvest wreath by sticking the seed pods, dried flowers, pine cones, and other natural materials onto the cardboard base using the glue gun. If you have younger children, use the glue gun yourself and let the children position the materials on the wreath. Carefully supervise older children.

3. As the children make their harvest wreaths, talk about the abundance of food that God has provided for us in nature. Ask the children to think of some of the plants we eat. Remind them that foods such as bread, rice, pasta, sugar, coffee, and breakfast cereals all come from plants.

BIBLE READING
Genesis 1:29-30
Isaiah 30:23

TIME REQUIRED
40 minutes

MATERIALS
hot glue gun

dried flowers, leaves, seed pods, grasses, pine cones

thick cardboard

scissors

clear spray varnish (gloss)

paintbrushes

4. **W**hen the wreaths are complete, plan to varnish them in a well-ventilated room without the children present. Let the wreaths dry thoroughly before letting the children take them home.

5. **C**onclude by inviting the children to go outside with you (if the weather is suitable) to enjoy the natural environment. Stand in a circle and ask each child in turn to name a food they especially want to thank God for providing. Conclude by praying together.

CRAFT VARIATION

Use colored paper, posterboard, or fabric to make leaves, fruits, and bright flowers.

42. BOOKMARK
STUDYING GOD'S WORD

This colorful bookmark will be useful for Bible study or marking special passages.

PREPARATION

Cut cardstock into rectangles measuring 6- by 2-inches. You will need one for each child.

1. Read the Bible verse to the children. Explain that the Bible is God's Word and is a gift to us from God. Although it was written by ordinary people, God inspired the writers' thoughts through the Holy Spirit. Ask if anyone has a favorite Bible passage or verse that they would like to share with the class. Discuss how the Bible shows us the way to lead a good life that will bring us happiness. It helps us make wise decisions. We should turn to the Bible whenever we want advice or guidance. Explain that the Bible outlines God's purpose and plans for us and tells us how to please God. We can get to know God by reading the Bible, and this will bring us closer to God.

2. Give out the craft materials for the children to make a bookmark to use in their Bibles at home. Have each child write on one side of the bookmark, "My favorite Bible verse is" and then write the relevant chapter and verse. Have a Bible and a Bible Concordance available if the children need help to look up the verse.

3. Let the children glue their photo on the other side of the bookmark. Suggest they sign their name and write the date under their photo. Help the children cover their bookmarks with clear contact paper. Punch a hole in the end of each bookmark. Cut ribbon into 6-inch pieces. Show the children how to tie the ribbon through the hole.

4. As the children make their bookmarks, talk about the value of reading the Bible and how understanding the Bible helps us. Remind the children that the Bible is God's Word.

BIBLE READING
Psalm 119:105

TIME REQUIRED
30 minutes

MATERIALS
Bible

Bible Concordance

cardstock
(assorted colors)

scissors

pencils

colored markers

small (school-size)
photo of each child

white glue

paper punch

ribbon in several
colors

clear contact paper

Ask the children to give you examples of the things the Bible teaches us:

- The Bible tells us who God is and how God relates to people.
- The Bible develops our faith and brings us closer to God.
- The Bible helps us to solve our problems.
- The Bible gives us peace of mind.
- The Bible offers good advice and helps to form our character.

4. Encourage the children to become familiar with the Bible by reading it daily. Suggest they find a quiet place to read so they can read, think, and pray as they learn God's Word. Ask a volunteer to read the prayer.

PRAYER

Wonderful God, we thank you for your Word. Be with us each day as we grow in our faith and learn more about you. Amen.

43. BANDANNA
BEING UNITED THROUGH JESUS

Making these bandannas is a great way for children to learn about being united with God through Jesus.

PREPARATION

Cut the fabric into 24-inch squares. You will need a square for each child. Hem the squares prior to the lesson.

1. Ask a volunteer to read the Bible verse to the children. Explain that our faith becomes stronger as we meet each week to learn about God and Jesus. This "togetherness" makes us part of God's family, through our belief in Jesus. It also unites us with the other members of our church family and churches around the world.

2. Invite the children to make bandannas to show unity with each other and with God. Distribute the pens and paper. Suggest that the children design their bandanna logo on paper before using fabric. They might like to discuss and plan their designs together. They could draw small crosses, hearts with "Jesus" written in the center, angels, the Lord's Prayer, or perhaps a Bible verse. Some might prefer a slogan, such as, "God Rules" or "JC4ME." Allow about twenty minutes for this part of the activity.

3. When the children are happy with their designs on paper, they can transfer them onto fabric. Give each child a fabric square and distribute the fabric markers. Caution the children to keep the markers away from their clothes.

4. As the children make their bandannas, explain that we are united with God by believing in Jesus and accepting Jesus as our Savior. We can strengthen our unity by regularly attending church and Sunday school, studying the Bible, learning how to please God, and spending time with other believers.

BIBLE READING
Galatians 3:26

TIME REQUIRED
40 minutes

MATERIALS
cotton fabric
(must be light colored)

fabric markers

paper and pens

5. When everyone has completed a bandanna, show them how to put it on. Suggest they wear it to the class each week. Invite the children to stand in a circle and hold hands with each other to symbolize being joined together in faith. Conclude by reading the prayer together.

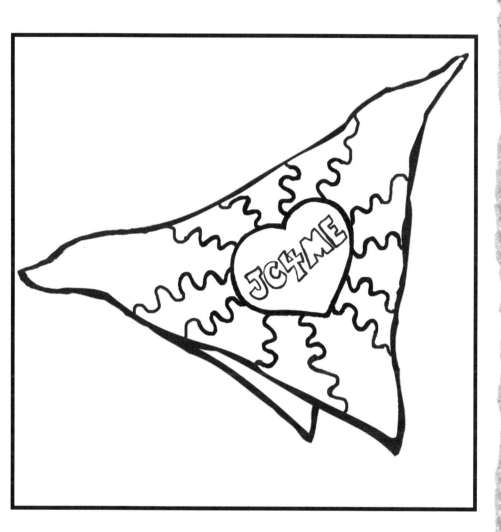

PRAYER

Dear God, we come to you together through Jesus Christ. Please help us to stay united with each other and with you. Amen.

44. DOOR HANGER
KNOWING GOD IS ALWAYS WITH US

This useful door hanger helps children to remember that God is always with us.

PREPARATION

Cut colored cardstock into 4- by 10-inch rectangles. Cut a hole at one end to fit over a standard door knob. (Option: plain wooden door hangers can be purchased from large craft shops.)

1. Choose a volunteer to read the Bible passage to the class. Explain that it tells us whenever we need God, God is with us. When we want to talk to God about our worries, God welcomes us and would never close the door on us. It is like having a best friend who is always at home when we knock on the door.

2. God wants to have a close and loving relationship with us. We can achieve this by sharing our lives with God every day. For example we can:
- tell God everything and be completely honest;
- give thanks and praise in our prayers;
- trust God to help us and take care of us;
- learn about God by reading the Bible and attending church.

3. Explain that when we do these things, we grow closer to God. It is rewarding to have quiet, personal time with God. Ask the children to think about having time with God while they make door hangers for their bedroom doors. Distribute the door hangers, colored markers, glue sticks, glitter glue, foil stars, sequins, and stickers. Ask the children to help you think of slogans to write on the door hangers. Copy their suggestions on a large piece of paper. If the children need help, suggest:

BIBLE READING
Matthew 7:7-8

TIME REQUIRED
40 minutes

MATERIALS
colored cardstock (or plain wooden door hangers)

scissors

colored markers

clear contact paper

glue sticks

glitter glue, sequins, foil stars and stickers (to decorate)

large piece of paper

- Quiet please! Prayer in progress.
- Come back later. I'm talking to God.
- Please knock! It's my prayer time.

When they have finished decorating them, cover the hangers with clear contact paper, and trim them neatly. Some children may need help with the contact paper.

4. **A**ssure the children that God's door is always open to them, and that God is waiting to hear their prayers. Conclude by reading the prayer to the class.

Cut here to hang around door knob.

Cut hole for door knob.

Quiet Please! Prayer In Progress

colored cardstock, 10" long and 4" wide

45. KEYCHAIN
JESUS, THE KEY TO SALVATION

This useful keychain is a reminder that Jesus is the key to salvation.

1. Ask the children to imagine they have a treasure chest full of gold and precious things. What would they need to open the chest and reach the treasure? They would need a key. Explain that we can liken the treasure to God, with Jesus being the key that opens the way to God.

2. Choose a volunteer to read the Bible verse to the class. Explain that Jesus is the way to God because he is the truth— Jesus is the personal self-revelation of God. Jesus is the life because he is the power that sustains humankind on their way to God. Jesus says that he alone is the way to the Father. Only by believing in Jesus can we receive everlasting life from God. Our faith in Jesus, our Savior, is the key to salvation.

3. Invite the children to make a special keychain as a reminder of this. Give each child a small lump of dough. Show them how to roll it out to about 2 inches wide and high, and ¼-inch thick. Show the children how to cut out the shape of the letter "**J**," using the plastic knives. Use a wooden skewer to make a small hole in the center of the horizontal part of the "**J**," where the keychain can be attached. The skewers can also be used to make patterns on the dough. Have the children paint the **J**'s they made. Line a tray with baking paper and carefully place the **J**'s on the baking trays. Write each child's name beside his or her **J** so that the children will be able to identify their own work.

4. When the children have finished making their keychains, ask them to sit quietly for a few moments. Encourage them to think about accepting Jesus as their Savior. After a few minutes, ask the children what it means to them to accept Jesus as our Savior. Do not insist if any of the children

BIBLE READING
John 14:6

TIME REQUIRED
40 minutes

MATERIALS

play dough
(see recipe)

plastic knives

ball keychains
(available from craft
stores)

acrylic paints

paintbrushes

wooden skewers

rolling pins

baking trays

baking paper

do not wish to share. Help the children to understand that accepting Jesus as our Savior means we will

    love God with all our hearts, our minds, and our souls

    try to follow Jesus' teachings

    pray, read the Bible, and attend worship

    associate with other Christians

    share the good news of Jesus and of God's love with others

5. Invite the children to pray with you. Allow time for the children to add their own personal prayers.

6. Bake the "J"s for eight hours at the lowest possible oven temperature. Varnish both sides. Allow time for the varnish to dry before helping the children attach the keychains.

PRAYER

Dear God, thank you for your Son, Jesus. Thank you for loving us and guiding us. Helps us to grow as Christians each day. Amen.

PLAY DOUGH RECIPE
Ingredients

10 cups flour

5 cups salt

5 cups water

Combine the ingredients in a food processor. If making by hand, add the water gradually to produce a soft, pliable consistency. This dough keeps in the refrigerator for one week in an airtight container. This quantity should be sufficient for a group of fifteen children.

46. KEEPSAKE JAR

GOD'S GIFTS

This keepsake jar is a reminder of the wonderful gifts we receive from God.

BIBLE READING
James 1:17

TIME REQUIRED
30 minutes

MATERIALS

clean jars with lids
(one for each child)

dried leaves

feathers

shells

dried flower heads

gold foil

pictures cut from
magazines of
homes, pets, people
laughing, and so forth

acrylic paints
(assorted colors)

paintbrushes

large piece of paper

1. Ask a volunteer to read the Bible verse to the class. Tell the children that we know God loves us because of the good things God gives us. Ask the children to suggest some. Write their responses on a large piece of paper. Be certain they include families, church, school, and friends. Encourage them to think of less tangible things too, like happy memories or a sunny day.

2. Explain that a keepsake jar can be a reminder of God's gifts to them. Brainstorm some things that could go in it. If the children need suggestions to get started, mention items such as shells to remember a happy vacation at the beach; feathers to represent beautiful birds; pictures of people to represent families and friendship; gold foil to represent sunlight. Ask the children for ideas of extra things to put in their jars as a reminder of God's good gifts.

3. Spread out the materials so the children have easy access to everything they need. Encourage them to think creatively about God's gifts before filling their jars. As the children fill their jars, talk about some of the gifts God gives us as individuals, such as

God's constant love

the promise of everlasting life

God's guidance in the Bible

knowing we can trust God

God's presence in our lives

the comfort we find in prayer

God's forgiveness when we make mistakes

4. **W**hen the jars are filled, invite the children to decorate them. Suggest they paint one of God's gifts, such as the sun, their home, or bright flowers on the lid and sides of the jar. When they have finished, allow a few minutes for the children to hold their jars and reflect on the good things God has given them. Ask everyone to think of one thing they are thankful for. Ask everyone to be ready to name those gifts during the prayer. Incorporate the children's suggestions into the prayer.

PRAYER
Loving Father,
we are thankful for
the wonderful gifts
you give us,
especially. . . .
*(Let the children add
their own thanks.)*
Amen.

47. FAITH JEWELRY
DECLARING YOUR FAITH

This clay jewelry is created as a way of letting others know one has faith in God.

1. Ask a volunteer to read the Bible verse to the children. Ask the children what the verse tells us about faith. Ask them what they think it means to have faith in God. Explain that it means to be certain of God's existence, even though we cannot see God. We know God exists because we have the Bible that tells us all about God. God wants everyone to know God and have true faith in God.

2. Ask the children to think of ways we can show our faith to other people. Explain that some people choose to wear a cross necklace or symbolic bracelet as a sign of their faith. Tell the children that they can make clay jewelry, a necklace or bracelet, to show their belief in God. Distribute a small amount of air-drying clay to each child (a piece the size of a golf ball is sufficient). Show them how to break off small pieces and roll them into round beads. Hand out the skewers and demonstrate how to push the stick through the center of the bead carefully to make a hole. Continue in this way until each child has made enough beads for his or her necklace or bracelet.

3. The next step is to give the beads a base color with the acrylic paints. Let the children choose their own colors, and paint the beads. While the beads are drying, ask everyone to think about what they would like to write or draw on the beads. Some suggestions are: I believe, God 4 Me, Faithful, God = life, or drawings of hearts, crosses, or doves. Distribute the fine-tipped paintbrushes and markers for the children to decorate their beads. Once dry, thread the beads with elastic thread. Tie the ends of the thread in a knot to secure.

BIBLE READING
Hebrews 11:1

TIME REQUIRED
40 minutes

MATERIALS
air-drying clay

elastic thread

wooden skewers

acrylic paints
(assorted colors)

white glue

paintbrushes
(small and fine-tipped)

fine-point permanent
markers

scissors

4. As the children make their jewelry, emphasize the importance of letting God know we have faith in God. We can do this through

 prayer

 reading the Bible

 following Jesus

 putting God above everything else

 worship

 trusting God and accepting the plans God has for our lives

 attending church and Sunday school

Ask the children for more suggestions.

5. Display the prayer and read it aloud together.

NOTE

The clay jewelry will take twenty-four hours to dry at room temperature.

PRAYER

Wonderful God, we believe in you and want others to know you too. Please help us to share our faith. Amen.

48. SCROLL
MAKING A COMMITMENT TO GOD

With this scroll, children can create a work of art and think about making a commitment to God.

BIBLE READING
John 15:4-5

TIME REQUIRED
40 minutes

MATERIALS
mock parchment paper (see preparation)

paintbrushes (fine-tipped)

gold acrylic paint

colored markers

red ribbon (one 8-inch piece per child)

large piece of paper

PREPARATION

To make the mock parchment paper for the scrolls, soak white paper in tea or coffee until it stains. Place the wet paper on a pad of recycled newspaper and iron until dry. Option: Purchase printer paper that looks like parchment.

1. Ask a volunteer to read the Bible passage. Ask the children what they think God is trying to tell us in this passage. The verse uses the words "fruit," "branches," and "vine;" but it is not talking about plants. Explain that staying joined to God is about being committed to God and living to please God. When we commit ourselves to God, we are asking God to be involved in every part of our lives. In return, we are promising to serve God, follow God's teaching, and remain faithful to God. We can strengthen our commitment and grow closer to God by talking to God in prayer, learning about God in the Bible, and regularly attending church and Sunday school.

2. Distribute the materials for the craft to the children and invite them to make a scroll. Explain that the scroll will be like a declaration of faith that they can sign if they choose to.

3. Encourage the children to write their own declarations, but write these suggestions on a large piece of paper for them to use as a model: I *(put your name here)* declare that I will find out what the Bible says about God and life and me. Or suggest: I *(name)* promise that I will faithfully follow the teaching of the Bible, and I will commit myself to serving God.

4. Let the children use colored markers to write on their scrolls in decorative lettering. When they have finished, suggest that they use the gold paint and fine-tipped brushes to outline and enhance capital letters and paint a border around the edges of the scroll.

5. When the children have finished creating their scrolls, talk about the things they can do to keep their declaration. Encourage the children to display their scrolls in a prominent place at home as a reminder of their commitment to God. Ask a volunteer to read the prayer.

6. When the paint is completely dry on the scrolls, roll them up, and tie a piece of red ribbon around each one.

CRAFT VARIATION
Use a computer to print out a choice of declarations in fancy fonts so the children only have to decorate rather than write.

49. CLAY SCULPTURE
HOW GOD SEES US

Clay is wonderful for expressing creativity. This sculpting craft can help children understand how valuable they are to God.

1. Write the words "God loves me just as I am" on a large piece of paper. Encourage the children to say it aloud as a group and then to each other. Explain that it is an important message to remember, because God does not judge us by our looks or by our weaknesses. God understands who we are and loves us individually. God created us, with our different personalities, appearances, talents, and abilities. To God, we are all important and valuable. Choose two volunteers to read the Bible verses to the class.

2. Invite the children to make a clay sculpture of themselves. It will be a head and shoulders sculpture. Give everyone a piece of clay the size of a tennis ball, a rolling pin, and modeling tools or plastic knives.

3. The easiest way to make this craft is to roll the clay out to ½-inch thickness on wax paper. Use a knife to cut out the shape of a head, neck, and shoulders. Use the remaining clay to make hair and features. Alternatively, the children can make a three-dimensional head and shoulders, then mould the features. Allow about twenty minutes for this part.

4. As the children work on their sculptures, ask them to think about the following questions:
- What do I like most about myself?
- Why am I special to God?
- What makes me happy?
- How do I please God?

BIBLE READING
Psalm 139:1-2
1 Samuel 16:7

TIME REQUIRED
40 minutes

MATERIALS
air-drying clay

modeling tools
(or plastic knives)

acrylic paints
(assorted colors)

paintbrushes
(selection of sizes)

rolling pins

wax paper

large piece of paper

5. When the children have finished, distribute the paints and paintbrushes for them to paint their sculptures. Allow about ten minutes for this. Display the statues for everyone to view. Ask a volunteer to read the prayer to the class.

NOTE

The sculptures will take twenty-four hours to dry at room temperature.

face, neck, and shoulders, cut from clay, all one piece

features cut from clay and placed on top

50. 3-D CARD
TELLING FRIENDS ABOUT JESUS

This attractive greeting card doubles as an invitation for friends to attend church and creates an opportunity for the children to think about sharing their faith.

BIBLE READING

Philippians 2:1-5

TIME REQUIRED

40 minutes

MATERIALS

blank cards (sold in packs and available from craft stores)

glue sticks

colored markers

tissue paper (assorted colors)

scissors

scraps of crafting foam, fur fabric, and felt

pencils

colored paper

large piece of paper

1. Ask a volunteer to read the Bible passage aloud. Ask the children what the Scripture tells us about Jesus. Encourage them to share what they discovered. Explain that many people have not heard these things about Jesus. They have not had the chance to know how good it is to live a life of faith with Jesus as their friend.

2. Talk with the class about how their friends, or other children they know, could be given the chance to find out about Jesus. Plan a special Sunday school event, where the children will have the opportunity to talk about their faith with the guests and tell them about Jesus and how believing in him brings us to God.

3. Decide on a date for this special event. Discuss what the children would like to do, such as showing a video about Jesus and serving some refreshments. Write the details on a large piece of paper. Explain that they can make a greeting card that will be an invitation for a friend to attend the special event.

4. Give everyone a card and let them create a picture on the front. Suggest they draw the outline first, then make it three dimensional with the other materials. For example, they could draw a dog and use fur fabric on the body. Or they could make tissue paper flowers on felt stalks. Allow about twenty minutes for this. Ask the children to think about the friend they would like to invite. Encourage them to write a personal message inside the card and give details about the special event. Help with spelling and grammar as needed.

5. **A**s the children make their cards, discuss what it means to have Jesus as our friend. When we believe in Jesus

　　we have a new start in life

　　we know God loves us

　　we know God forgives us

　　we know God protects us

　　we belong to to the family of God

　　we have the promise of everlasting life

　　we know that God is always with us

Ask the children for more suggestions.

6. **W**hen the cards are completed, ask a volunteer to read the prayer. Encourage the children to pray for their friends.

PRAYER

Lord, help us to bring our friends to learn about you, so that they may be part of your family too. Amen.

BIBLE REFERENCES

Honesty - Leviticus 19:11, Ephesians 4:25
Obeying God - 1 John 2:3, Psalm 86:11, John 15:10
Good behavior - Philippians 2:14-15, Luke 6:31
Helping others - Galatians 6:10, Romans 15:1-2
Obeying parents - Ephesians 6:1, Exodus 20:12
Reading the Bible - Psalm 32:8, Psalm 119:105, 2 Timothy 3:16-17
Forgiveness - Matthew 6:14-15, Colossians 3:13, Mark 11:25-26
Witnessing - Matthew 28:19-20, Mark 16:15, 1 Peter 3:15
Showing love - 1 Corinthians 13:4-8, Galatians 5:14, 1 John 4:19
Attending church - Hebrews 10:25, 1 Corinthians 12:27
Worrying - Philippians 4:7, 1 Peter 5:7
Trusting God - Proverbs 3:5-6, James 1:5, Isaiah 26:3-4
Kindness - Colossians 3:12, Ephesians 4:32
Prayer - 1 Thessalonians 5:17-18, Matthew 6:9-13
Giving/sharing - Matthew 5:42, 2 Corinthians 9:7

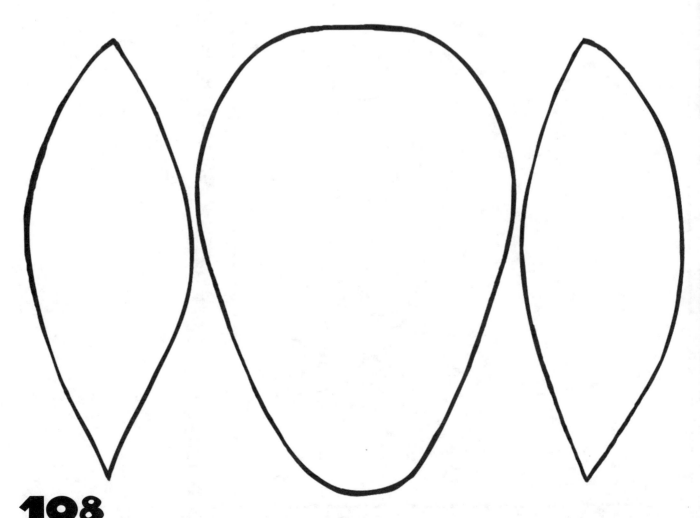

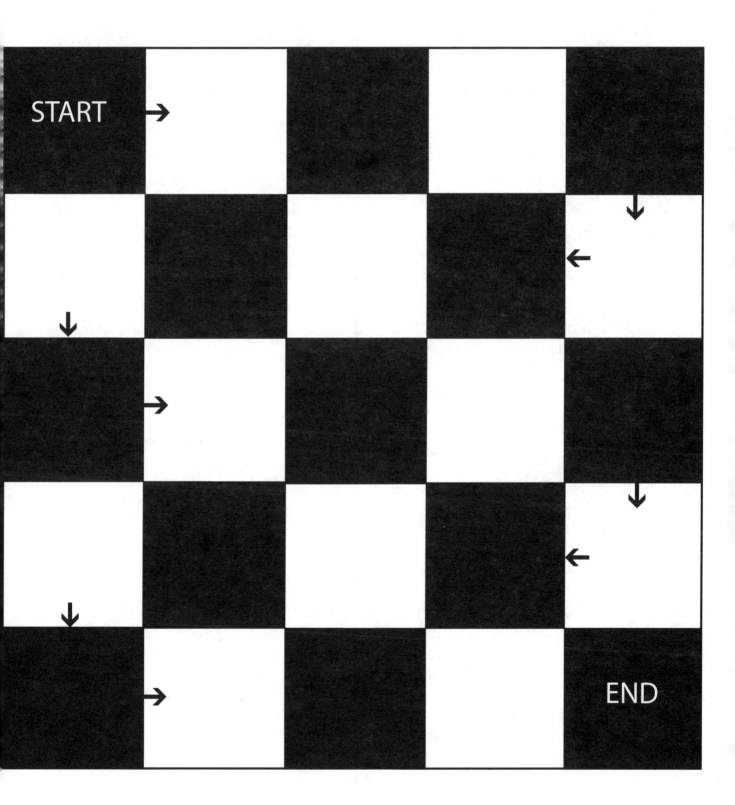

START →

END

109

BIRD FEEDING GUIDE

SEEDS

You can use a mixture of these seeds in your birdfeeder:

Cracked corn for doves, jays, sparrows

Hulled sunflower for cardinals, jays, finches, chickadees, goldfinches

Safflower for sparrows, doves, cardinals

Black sunflower for cardinals, finches, titmice, grosbeaks, chickadees

Striped sunflower for jays, cardinals, titmice, grosbeaks

Thistle for finches

FRUIT

Apple, pear, kiwi fruit, peaches, plums, figs, cranberries for robins, catbirds, orioles, tanagers, redwings

IMPORTANT

Birds will be especially in need of food throughout the winter months. Remember to fill your feeder regularly. Make sure your feeder is out of the reach of cats and dogs so that the birds can feed safely.

BIRD FEEDING GUIDE

SEEDS

You can use a mixture of these seeds in your birdfeeder:

Cracked corn for doves, jays, sparrows

Hulled sunflower for cardinals, jays, finches, chickadees, goldfinches

Safflower for sparrows, doves, cardinals

Black sunflower for cardinals, finches, titmice, grosbeaks, chickadees

Striped sunflower for jays, cardinals, titmice, grosbeaks

Thistle for finches

FRUIT

Apple, pear, kiwi fruit, peaches, plums, figs, cranberries for robins, catbirds, orioles, tanagers, redwings

IMPORTANT

Birds will be especially in need of food throughout the winter months. Remember to fill your feeder regularly. Make sure your feeder is out of the reach of cats and dogs so that the birds can feed safely.

111

112